What Others Are Saying

The future is Electric is a timely treatise in the highly disruptive EV revolution, where questions far outweigh answers.

In his simple to read, yet highly informative book, Ingemar Anderson takes us on an in-depth analysis of how to maneuver this unexpected rapid transportation upheaval, providing an easy-to-read blueprint of what is going on, how it affects us, relieving any anxiety that this transition is good for humankind, and how we can embrace it, and be part of it.

It is both an enlightening book and will become a reference manual in your library after reading.

—Pete Gruber, Gruber Motor Company,
The first commercial independent Tesla Service

THE FUTURE IS ELECTRIC

THE MOST COMPLETE GUIDE TO THE WORLD OF EVS AND BEYOND

The Future is Electric
The Most Complete Guide to the World of EVs and Beyond

First Edition, Published 2023

By Ingemar Anderson

Cover Design and Interior Layout by Reprospace, LLC
Translated into German, Spanish, and Portugese by www.DeepL.com

Research and writing supported by OpenAI.com, ChatGPT
Artwork created by Midjourney.com
Edited by www.Grammarly.com

Paperback ISBN-13: 978-1-952685-60-6

KITSAP
PUBLISHING

Published by Kitsap Publishing
www.KitsapPublishing.com

Dedication

To all those who believe that a cleaner, more sustainable future is possible, and who are willing to take action to make it a reality. May this guide inspire you to learn about and embrace the power of electric vehicles, and may it help to guide you towards a more sustainable future for ourselves and for generations to come.

Acknowledgments

I would like to express my deepest gratitude to everyone who has supported me in the creation of this book.

First and foremost, I want to thank my family and friends for their unwavering support and encouragement throughout this journey. Your words of encouragement and inspiration kept me going through the long hours of research and writing.

I would also like to extend a heartfelt thanks to the countless electric vehicle experts and enthusiasts who have generously shared their knowledge and expertise with me. Without your insights, this book would not have been possible.

I would like to express my gratitude to the team at OpenAI for their valuable contribution to this book. Their ChatGPT tool has provided me extensive research and text, which helped to shape and enrich the content of this book. Without their efforts, this book would not have been possible. Thank you for your dedication to advancing the field of artificial intelligence and making innovative tools available to writers and researchers.

Finally, I want to thank the readers of this book, for your interest in and commitment to the future of sustainable transportation. It is my hope that this guide will inspire you to learn more about EVs, and to take action towards a more sustainable and equitable future for all.

Ingemar Alexander Anderson

CONTENTS

THE FUTURE

APPENDIX

My first electric car was a 2018 Nissan Leaf (Author Picture)

Foreword

This book is an excellent resource for anyone new to electric cars
and who wants to learn

"I think it's important to have a future that is electric, and it's important that we think about sustainable transport." —Elon Musk in an interview with The Telegraph, 2013

Pete Gruber - Gruber Motor Company

The future is Electric is a timely treatise in the highly disruptive EV revolution, where questions far outweigh answers.

In his simple to read, yet highly informative book, Ingemar Anderson takes us on an in-depth analysis of how to maneuver this unexpected rapid transportation upheaval, providing an easy-to-read blueprint of what is going on, how it affects us, relieving any anxiety that this transition is good for humankind, and how we can embrace it, and be part of it.

It is both an enlightening book and will become a reference manual in your library after reading.

From the Author

Welcome to *The Future is Electric*, a comprehensive guide to understanding and embracing the future of sustainable transportation. I'm thrilled to see more people interested in electric cars and the benefits they offer, from cleaner air to reduced dependence on fossil fuels.

I believe that electric cars are the way forward for the automotive industry, and I've dedicated much time to promoting this technology. It's exciting to see how far we've come, but much work must be done to accelerate the transition to sustainable energy.

This book is an excellent resource for anyone new to electric cars and who wants to learn more. The author has provided a clear and concise overview of the technology, its benefits, and its challenges. He covers everything from how electric cars work to more advanced topics like charging infrastructure and maintenance.

The Future is Electric is more than just a guide; it's a call to action. We need everyone to understand the importance of electric cars and embrace them as a critical solution to the global climate crisis. We need to work together to build a cleaner, more sustainable future.

This book will inspire you to join the movement toward electric cars and become an advocate for sustainable transportation. Let's work together to create a better world for ourselves and future generations.

Introduction

"By 2030, electric vehicles will account for 50% of new car sales, and by 2040, they will make up more than a third of the world's fleet."
—Bloomberg New Energy Finance

The future is electric for several reasons, primarily due to the environmental benefits and technological advancements of electric vehicles.

One of the most significant reasons that the future is electric is the urgent need to reduce greenhouse gas emissions and combat climate change. Transportation is a major contributor to global emissions, and switching to electric vehicles can significantly reduce our carbon footprint and help us transition to a more sustainable energy system.

In addition to their environmental benefits, electric vehicles offer several other advantages over traditional gasoline-powered vehicles. Electric cars are more efficient, quieter, and require less maintenance, which can save drivers time and money in the long run. They also offer instant torque and a smooth driving experience, making them fun and practical to drive.

As battery technology continues to improve and the cost of EVs comes down, more and more people are likely to make the switch to electric cars. This will in turn drive further innovation and investment in the EV industry, leading to even greater efficiency and performance gains.

Finally, electric vehicles are a key component of the larger shift towards renewable energy sources and a more sustainable energy system. As we transition to more wind, solar, and other forms of clean energy, electric vehicles will become an increasingly important part of the grid, providing a flexible and reliable means of storing and using renewable energy.

Electric vehicles offer a cleaner, more efficient, and more sustainable alternative to traditional gasoline-powered cars. As more people embrace the benefits of EVs, the future of transportation will become cleaner, more efficient, and more sustainable for everyone. Electric cars are changing the way we think about transportation. With advancements in technology and the increasing awareness of the need for sustainable living, more and more people are considering electric cars as a viable option. However, making the switch to electric can be daunting, especially for those who are new to the world of electric cars. This book aims to take away any concerns and answer all questions that beginners may have about electric cars.

From the history of electric cars to how they work, this book will cover everything a beginner needs to know. We'll explore the environmental and economic benefits of owning an electric car, as well as provide practical tips for charging and maintaining an electric car. Additionally, we'll address some common concerns about electric cars, such as their range and reliability, and provide real-world examples of electric car ownership to give readers a better understanding of what it's like to own and drive one.

By the end of this book, readers will have a comprehensive understanding of electric cars and be equipped with the knowledge to make an informed decision about whether an electric car is right for them.

PART ONE

PRELUDE

A woman in 1908 uses a hand-cranked battery charger to charge her electric Columbia Mark 68 Victoria automobile. The Pope Manufacturing Company made such a car in 1906 and the charger in 1912.

CHAPTER 1

The History of Electric Cars

In this chapter, we'll delve into the history of electric cars, from their inception to their rise in popularity in the 21st century. We'll discuss how electric cars have evolved over time, the key figures who helped shape the electric car industry, and the role of government and environmental regulations in promoting electric cars. By the end of this chapter, readers will have a better understanding of how electric cars have developed and why they are becoming an increasingly important part of the transportation landscape.

Electric cars may seem like a modern innovation, but in fact, the idea of electric vehicles has been around for more than a century. From the first electric cars in the 1800s to the recent surge in popularity, the history of electric cars is a fascinating journey through innovation, creativity, and perseverance.

EARLY ELECTRIC CARS

The earliest electric cars were developed in the mid-19th century, shortly after the invention of the battery. These early cars were slow, heavy, and had a limited range, but they were seen as a promising alternative to the noisy, smelly, and unreliable gasoline cars of the time.

One of the first electric cars was built by Thomas Davenport, an American inventor, in 1834. His car was powered by a series of batteries and could travel up to 12 miles per hour. In 1884, Thomas Parker, a British inventor, built the first practical electric car, which was powered by lead-acid batteries.

ELECTRIC CARS IN THE 20TH CENTURY

In the early 20th century, electric cars became more popular, especially among women, who appreciated their quiet and clean operation. Many car companies, including Baker, Columbia, and Detroit Electric, produced electric cars that were used for city driving and short trips.

In 1912, a Detroit Electric car set a new record by traveling 211 miles on a single charge. Electric cars were also popular in Europe, where they were used as taxis and delivery vehicles.

However, the rise of gasoline cars, which had longer ranges and were easier to refuel, led to a decline in the popularity of electric cars. The invention of the electric starter for gasoline cars in 1912 also made gasoline cars more convenient to operate.

ELECTRIC CARS IN THE MODERN ERA

In the 1960s and 1970s, electric cars experienced a resurgence, fueled by concerns over air pollution and the high price of gasoline during the oil crisis. In 1966, General Motors introduced the Electrovair, an experimental electric car that used a modified Corvair chassis and a 115-horsepower electric motor.

In the 1990s, California implemented new regulations that required car companies to produce a certain number of zero-emission vehicles (ZEVs), including electric cars. This led to the development of electric cars by several major car companies, including General Motors, Toyota, and Nissan.

The first mass-produced electric car was the General Motors EV1, which was released in 1996. The EV1 was a two-seater car that had a range of up to 140 miles and could be charged in eight hours. However, GM discontinued the EV1 in 2003, citing low demand and high production costs.

In the 2000s, the development of lithium-ion batteries and advances in electric motor technology led to a new wave of electric cars. Tesla, a Silicon Valley startup founded by Elon Musk, introduced the Roadster, a high-performance electric sports car, in 2008. The Roadster had a range of up to 245 miles and could go from 0 to 60 mph in 3.7 seconds.

Since then, Tesla has become a leader in the electric car industry, producing a range of electric cars that have pushed the boundaries of range, performance, and design. Other car companies, including Nissan, BMW, and Chevrolet, have also introduced electric cars that are more practical and affordable for everyday drivers.

CONCLUSION

The history of electric cars is a story of innovation, setbacks, and progress. While electric cars have faced many challenges over the years, including limited range, high production costs, and low demand, they continue to gain popularity as a more sustainable and efficient form of transportation.

CHAPTER 2

How Electric Cars Work

""I am most excited for the advent of electric cars. Tesla is really changing the game." —**Richard Branson**

In this chapter, we'll explore the basic components of an electric car, including the battery, electric motor, and charging system. We'll explain the difference between all-electric and hybrid electric cars, and provide an overview of the benefits of each. Additionally, we'll address common concerns about electric cars, such as their range, charging times, and driving experience, and provide real-world examples of electric car ownership to help readers better understand what it's like to drive one.

We'll also delve into the fundamental components of electric cars, how they work, and the differences between all-electric and hybrid electric vehicles. We'll also address some of the common concerns that people have about electric cars and share real-world examples to help readers understand what it's like to own and drive one.

THE BATTERY

The battery is the heart of an electric car, providing the power needed to drive the electric motor. Electric car batteries are made up of hundreds or thousands of individual cells that are typically arranged in modules. The most common type of battery used in electric cars is a lithium-ion battery, which is similar to the batteries used in laptops and cell phones. Lithium-ion batteries are lightweight, energy-dense, and can be recharged hundreds or thousands of times before needing to be replaced.

The other type are solid-state batteries. They are a newer type of EV battery that are currently being developed and tested by several manufacturers. These batteries use a solid electrolyte instead of a liquid or gel electrolyte, which can provide a number of benefits such as higher energy density, faster charging times, and increased safety. However, solid-state batteries are currently more expensive to produce than lithium-ion batteries and are still in the early stages of development.

Lithium-ion batteries are made up of several raw materials, including:

- Lithium: This is the primary active material in the battery and is responsible for storing and releasing energy.
- Electrolyte: This is a liquid or gel substance that conducts ions between the battery's electrodes. It is typically made up of a mixture of solvents, salts, and additives.
- Cathode: This is the positive electrode in the battery and is typically made up of a variety of materials, such as lithium cobalt oxide, lithium nickel manganese cobalt oxide, or lithium iron phosphate.
- Anode: This is the negative electrode in the battery and is typically made up of graphite or silicon-based materials.
- Separator: This is a thin, porous material that sits between the cathode and anode and helps to prevent them from coming into contact with each other.

Other materials used in the production of lithium-ion batteries include binders, conductive additives, and current collectors. The exact materials used can vary depending on the specific battery design and application.

The most rare material that is required for an EV battery is typically considered to be *cobalt*. Cobalt is used in the cathodes of many lithium-ion batteries, including those used in electric vehicles. While cobalt is not necessarily the scarcest element on the planet, it is relatively rare and is primarily mined in a few countries, including the Democratic Republic of Congo, which can make it difficult and expensive to obtain. Additionally, there are concerns about the environmental and social impacts of cobalt mining, including issues related to labor practices and human rights abuses. As a result, many battery manufacturers are working to reduce their reliance on cobalt and are exploring alternative materials and battery chemistries that can help to mitigate these issues.

The availability of rare elements such as cobalt, lithium, and rare earth elements can potentially pose a threat to the production of electric vehicles, as these materials are essential for the manufacture of EV batteries and other key components. The supply of these materials is limited, and there are concerns about the environmental and social impacts of their extraction and production, particularly in countries with lax environmental and labor regulations. Additionally, as the demand for EVs continues to grow, there may be increased competition for these materials, which could drive up prices and create supply chain disruptions. To mitigate these risks, many EV manufacturers and battery suppliers are working to reduce their reliance on these materials and are exploring alternative battery chemistries and recycling technologies that can help to conserve these critical resources.

THE ELECTRIC MOTOR

The electric motor is what makes an electric car move. It works by converting electrical energy from the battery into mechanical energy that drives the wheels. Electric motors are more efficient than gasoline engines, which means they use less energy to travel the same distance. They are also quieter and produce no emissions.

Nicola Tesla (July 10, 1856—January 7, 1943) is credited with inventing the alternating current (AC) electric motor. The AC motor is a type of electric motor that uses alternating current to generate a rotating magnetic field, which in turn drives the rotation of a shaft. Nicola Tesla's invention of the AC motor was a significant advancement in electrical engineering and played a crucial role in the development of modern power systems. Today, AC motors are widely used in a variety of applications, from industrial machinery to household appliances and electric vehicles.

Tesla Inc. uses AC induction motors in its electric vehicles (EVs). The AC motor technology used by Tesla Inc. was inspired by Nikola Tesla's original invention of the AC induction motor. Tesla Inc's electric motors are specifically designed for EVs and offer high efficiency, reliability, and performance. The motors used in some Tesla models have a unique cylindrical design, which allows for better cooling and power density. Overall, Tesla's use of AC induction motor technology has been a significant factor in the success of their EVs and has helped to advance the adoption of electric vehicles around the world.

While many electric vehicles (EVs) use AC motors, the specific motor technology used by Tesla is proprietary and not used by other EV manufacturers. Other manufacturers may use their own proprietary AC motor technology or license technology from other companies. Additionally, some EVs use other types of electric motors, such as permanent magnet motors or induction motors, which have their own unique advantages and disadvantages. Ultimately, the choice of electric motor technology depends on various factors, including performance, efficiency, cost, and the specific needs of the vehicle and its intended use.

ALL-ELECTRIC VS. HYBRID ELECTRIC CARS

All-electric cars (also called battery electric vehicles or BEVs) run solely on electricity and have no gasoline engine. They rely entirely on the battery and electric motor to power the car. Hybrid electric cars (also called plug-in hybrid electric vehicles or PHEVs) have both an electric motor and a gasoline engine. They can run on electricity alone for a certain distance, but when the battery is depleted, the gasoline engine kicks in to extend the car's range.

THE SCHEMATICS OF AN ELECTRIC CAR

Overall, the schematics of an electric car are complex but essential to understanding how the car operates. The electrical system is what differentiates electric cars from traditional gas-powered cars, and it is the key to their performance, efficiency, and environmental benefits.

Rough schematics of an electric car showing the battery block under the seats and the motor between the rear wheels. Other components are inverter, converters, controllers.

BENEFITS OF ELECTRIC CARS

Electric cars provide a host of advantages compared to their gasoline-powered counterparts. Emitting zero pollutants, these eco-friendly vehicles contribute to a healthier environment and improved public health. Furthermore, they boast increased efficiency and, in the long run, prove more cost-effective to operate. The driving experience in an electric car is characterized by its hushed and seamless performance, and the convenience of home charging eliminates the hassle of frequenting gas stations.

COMMON CONCERNS ABOUT ELECTRIC CARS

Many people have concerns about electric cars, particularly when it comes to range, charging times, and driving experience. While electric cars may have a shorter range than some gasoline-powered cars, most modern electric cars can now travel 200-300 miles on a single charge. Charging times can also be a concern, but with the increasing availability of fast-charging stations, it is possible to recharge an electric car in as little as 30 minutes. Finally, while some people worry that electric cars may be less fun to drive, in reality, electric cars offer excellent acceleration and handling.

In conclusion, understanding the basic components of electric cars is an essential first step in embracing the future of sustainable transportation. With their efficient, emissions-free technology and quiet, smooth driving experience, electric cars offer many benefits over traditional gasoline-powered cars. By addressing common concerns and sharing real-world examples, we hope to inspire readers to consider electric cars as a viable option for their next vehicle.

CHAPTER 3

Economic Benefits of Electric Cars

In this chapter, we'll discuss the environmental and economic benefits of owning an electric car. We'll explore the reduction in greenhouse gas emissions that comes with driving an electric car, as well as the potential cost savings associated with owning one. We'll also provide an overview of government incentives and tax credits that are available to electric car owners.

ECONOMIC BENEFITS

Electric cars aren't just good for the environment, they're also good for your wallet. Here are a few of the ways that electric cars can save you money:

Lower Fuel Costs

One of the most obvious benefits of electric cars is that they don't require gasoline. Instead, they're powered by electricity, which is often cheaper than gasoline. Depending on where you live, the cost of charging an electric car can be significantly less than the cost of filling up a gas tank.

In addition, many utilities offer special rates for electric car owners, which can further reduce the cost of charging. Over the lifetime of an electric car, the savings on fuel costs can add up to thousands of dollars.

Lower Maintenance Costs

Electric cars have fewer moving parts than gasoline cars, which means they require less maintenance. There's no oil to change, no spark plugs to replace, and no exhaust system to repair. Electric cars also have regenerative braking, which means that the brake pads last longer.

While electric cars may require occasional maintenance on the battery and electric motor, these costs are typically lower than the cost of maintaining a gasoline engine. Overall, the lower maintenance costs of electric cars can save owners hundreds or even thousands of dollars over the life of the car.

Conclusion

So there you have it, folks. Electric cars aren't just good for the environment, they're also good for your wallet. With lower fuel costs, lower maintenance costs, tax incentives, and higher resale values, electric cars can save you money in a variety of ways.

As the technology behind electric cars continues to improve, we can expect even more economic benefits in the future. So if you're considering buying a new car, I strongly encourage you to take a look at electric cars. They're not just the right choice for the planet, they're also the right choice for your wallet.

GOVERNMENT INCENTIVES AND TAX CREDITS

Many governments offer tax incentives for electric car owners, which can further reduce the cost of owning an electric car. In the United States, for example, there is a federal tax credit of up to $7,500 for electric car buyers. Some states also offer additional incentives, such as rebates or tax credits.

In addition to these incentives, some cities and municipalities offer free or discounted parking for electric cars, as well as access to HOV lanes and toll roads.

Resale Value

Electric cars also tend to have higher resale values than gasoline cars. This is partly because electric cars are still a relatively new technology, and demand for them is growing. It's also because electric cars have lower maintenance costs and lower fuel costs, which make them more attractive to buyers.

ENVIRONMENTAL BENEFITS

Electric cars are not just a cool new toy for techies, they are a critical solution to the climate crisis. Here are a few ways that electric cars can help the environment:

Reduced Emissions

One of the most obvious benefits of electric cars is that they produce zero tailpipe emissions. This means that they don't release any harmful pollutants or greenhouse gases into the atmosphere. By driving an electric car, you can help to reduce air pollution and improve the quality of the air we breathe.

Even when taking into account the emissions from electricity generation, electric cars produce fewer emissions than gasoline cars over their lifetime. In fact, a study by the Union of Concerned Scientists found that in the United States, electric cars produce less than half the emissions of gasoline cars, even when the emissions from electricity generation are factored in.

Reduced Dependence on Fossil Fuels

Electric cars also help to reduce our dependence on fossil fuels. By using electricity as a fuel source, we can shift away from oil and gas, which are finite resources that contribute to climate change.

In addition, because electricity can be generated from a variety of sources, including solar, wind, and hydroelectric power, electric cars offer a way to transition to a cleaner, more sustainable energy system.

Reduced Noise Pollution

Finally, electric cars produce less noise pollution than gasoline cars. This is because electric motors are quieter than gasoline engines. This means that electric cars are a great choice for people who live in cities or near busy roads, where noise pollution can be a major problem.

Conclusion

So there you have it, folks. Electric cars offer a range of environmental benefits, from reduced emissions and dependence on fossil fuels to reduced noise pollution. By driving an electric car, you can help to create a cleaner, more sustainable future for ourselves and for future generations.

I truly believe that electric cars are the future of transportation, and I support making electric cars more affordable and accessible to people around the world. With your support, we can build a brighter future for ourselves and for the planet. Thank you for joining me on this journey!

PART TWO

EV OWNERSHIP

CHAPTER 4

Choosing the Right EV

In this chapter, we'll provide guidance on how to choose the right electric car for your needs. We'll discuss factors to consider, such as range, charging infrastructure, and cost, and provide an overview of the different models currently available on the market. Additionally, we'll address common concerns about electric cars, such as their reliability and performance, and provide real-world examples of electric car ownership to help readers make an informed decision.

TYPES OF ELECTRIC VEHICLES

- Battery Electric Vehicles (BEVs)
- Plug-in Hybrid Electric Vehicles (PHEVs)
- Hybrid Electric Vehicles (HEVs)
- Fuel Cell Electric Vehicles (FCEVs)

Electric cars are not one-size-fits-all, and there are different types of electric cars to suit different needs and preferences.

Here are a few of the types of electric cars that are available:

ALL-ELECTRIC CARS (BEV)

All-electric cars, also known as battery electric vehicles or BEVs, run entirely on electricity and have no gasoline engine. They are powered by a battery and electric motor and can be charged using a standard electrical outlet or a dedicated charging station. All-electric cars offer zero tailpipe emissions and are a great choice for people who want a car that is both clean and efficient.

PLUG-IN HYBRID ELECTRIC CARS (PHEV)

Hybrid electric cars, also known as plug-in hybrid electric vehicles or PHEVs, have both an electric motor and a gasoline engine. They can run on electricity alone for a certain distance, but when the battery is depleted, the gasoline engine kicks in to extend the car's range. Hybrid electric cars offer a balance between the efficiency and cleanliness of electric cars and the convenience of gasoline cars.

There are several examples of plug-in hybrid electric cars (PHEVs) available on the market today, including:

- Toyota Prius Prime: The Prius Prime is a PHEV version of the popular Toyota Prius hybrid, with an all-electric range of around 25 miles before the gasoline engine takes over.
- Ford Fusion Energi: The Fusion Energi is a midsize sedan that can drive up to 26 miles on electricity alone before the gas engine kicks in.
- BMW i3 REx: The i3 REx is a compact car that combines an electric motor with a small gasoline engine that acts as a range extender. It has an all-electric range of around 110 miles, with an additional 70 miles provided by the gasoline engine.
- Mitsubishi Outlander PHEV: The Outlander PHEV is an SUV that can drive up to 22 miles on electricity alone, and also features all-wheel drive and a gasoline engine for extended range.
- Volvo XC90 T8: The XC90 T8 is a luxury SUV with a plug-in hybrid powertrain that can drive up to 18 miles on electricity

alone, and features a powerful gasoline engine for extended range.

These are just a few examples of the many PHEVs available on the market today, with more models expected to be released in the coming years as automakers continue to invest in electric and hybrid technology.

HYBRID ELECTRIC VEHICLES (HEV)

Hybrid Electric Vehicles (HEVs) are vehicles that combine a traditional internal combustion engine (usually gasoline) with an electric motor and battery. The electric motor and battery work in tandem with the gasoline engine to improve fuel efficiency and reduce emissions.

There are two main types of HEVs: series hybrids and parallel hybrids. In a series hybrid, the gasoline engine powers a generator that charges the battery, which then powers the electric motor that drives the wheels. In a parallel hybrid, the gasoline engine and electric motor are both connected to the transmission and can work together to power the vehicle.

HEVs offer several advantages over traditional gasoline-powered vehicles, including improved fuel efficiency, reduced emissions, and better performance. They also require less maintenance than gasoline-powered vehicles, since the electric motor can help reduce wear and tear on the gasoline engine.

HEVs are also an important transitional technology on the path towards fully electric vehicles (EVs). By incorporating electric power into a traditional gasoline-powered vehicle, HEVs help to familiarize consumers with electric drivetrains and provide a stepping stone towards full electrification.

There are several examples of hybrid electric vehicles (HEVs) available on the market today, including:

- Toyota Prius: The Prius is a compact hatchback that was the first mass-produced hybrid vehicle. It features a gasoline engine and electric motor that work together to provide improved fuel efficiency.
- Honda Insight: The Insight is a compact sedan that also features a gasoline engine and electric motor, and has been praised for its sporty handling and fuel efficiency.
- Ford Escape Hybrid: The Escape Hybrid is an SUV that combines a gasoline engine with an electric motor, and has been lauded for its comfortable ride and spacious interior.
- Hyundai Ioniq Hybrid: The Ioniq Hybrid is a compact hatchback that offers a stylish design, good fuel efficiency, and a range of advanced safety features.
- Kia Niro: The Niro is a hybrid SUV that offers a roomy interior and advanced safety features, and has been praised for its smooth ride and good handling.

These are just a few examples of the many HEVs available on the market today, with more models expected to be released in the coming years as automakers continue to invest in electric and hybrid technology.

EXTENDED-RANGE ELECTRIC CARS

Extended-range electric cars, also known as range-extended electric vehicles or REEVs, are similar to PHEVs but have a larger battery and a smaller gasoline engine. The gasoline engine is used only to generate electricity to power the electric motor, and the car can travel much farther on a single charge than a traditional PHEV. Extended-range electric cars offer the benefits of electric cars with the added security of a backup generator.

FUEL CELL CARS

Fuel cell cars, also known as hydrogen fuel cell vehicles or FCVs, are powered by electricity generated by a chemical reaction between hydrogen and oxygen. Fuel cell cars produce only water vapor as a byproduct and offer zero tailpipe emissions. However, they are currently less common than other types of electric cars and require access to hydrogen fueling stations.

So there you have it, folks. There are several different types of electric cars to choose from, depending on your needs and preferences. Whether you're looking for a car that is clean, efficient, or convenient, there is an electric car out there for you.

Currently, there are several FCEVs available on the market, including:

- Toyota Mirai: The Mirai is a mid-size sedan that uses fuel cells to power its electric motor. It has a range of around 312 miles and can be refueled in just a few minutes.
- Hyundai Nexo: The Nexo is a mid-size SUV that uses fuel cells to power its electric motor. It has a range of around 380 miles and can be refueled in just a few minutes.
- Honda Clarity Fuel Cell: The Clarity is a mid-size sedan that uses fuel cells to power its electric motor. It has a range of around 360 miles and can be refueled in just a few minutes.

FCEVs offer several advantages over traditional gasoline-powered vehicles and battery electric vehicles, including longer ranges and faster refueling times. However, the availability of hydrogen refueling stations is currently limited, which can make it difficult to use FCEVs as a primary mode of transportation in some areas. Nevertheless, FCEVs are seen as a promising technology for achieving a zero-emissions future, particularly in heavy-duty applications such as buses and trucks.

COMPARISON

All types of electric cars have their pros and cons, and the best type of electric car for you depends on your individual needs and preferences. All-electric cars, for example, offer zero tailpipe emissions and are very efficient, but today they may still not be the best option for people who need to travel long distances without access to charging. Hybrid electric cars, on the other hand, offer the convenience of gasoline engines with the efficiency of electric motors, but they still produce emissions and require more maintenance.

In terms of charging we should emphasize the importance of fast, convenient charging options. DC fast charging is the fastest and most convenient option for long-distance travel, but it can be expensive and may not be available in all areas. Level 2 charging is a good option for daily charging at home, while level 1 charging may be a good choice for people who don't drive long distances or who have access to charging at work or other locations.

Overall, we need to stress the importance of choosing an electric car that fits your individual needs and preferences, while also considering the environmental and economic benefits of electric cars. Auto companies constantly work to improve our electric cars and charging infrastructure to make electric cars more accessible and convenient for people around the world.

FACTORS TO CONSIDER WHEN CHOOSING AN EV

There are several factors to consider when choosing an electric car:

Range: Consider the range of the electric car and how it fits with your daily driving needs. If you have a long commute or frequently take long trips, you'll want a car with a longer range.

Charging: Consider the different types of charging options available and whether they fit with your lifestyle. If you have a reliable charging station at home or work, you may not need to worry about public charging stations as much. If you frequently travel long distances, DC fast charging may be important.

Cost: Consider the upfront cost of a car and how it fits with your budget. In 2023, electric cars will become less expensive than gasoline cars, and BEVs often have lower maintenance and fuel costs over the life of the car.

Performance: Consider the performance of the electric car and how it fits with your driving style. Electric cars can be very fast and efficient, and they are now becoming the best choice for people who prioritize high horsepower or towing capacity.

Environmental impact: Consider the environmental impact of the electric car and how it fits with your personal values. Electric cars produce zero tailpipe emissions, which can help to reduce air pollution and greenhouse gas emissions.

Brand and reputation: Consider the brand and reputation of the electric car manufacturer. Look for a company with a strong track record of innovation and quality, and one that is committed to improving the electric car industry as a whole.

> *Overall, choosing an electric car is a personal decision that depends on your individual needs and preferences. By considering these factors, you can make an informed decision and choose an electric car that is right for you.*

Factor	Gas Cars	BEVs
Range	Generally higher range, but varies by model and fuel efficiency	Varies by model, but typically lower range than gas cars
Charging	Refueling takes minutes, but requires access to gas stations	Charging takes longer, but can be done at home or public charging stations
Cost	Generally lower upfront cost, but higher fuel and maintenance costs over time	Generally higher upfront cost, but lower fuel and maintenance costs over time
Performance	Generally higher horsepower and towing capacity, but lower efficiency	Generally lower horsepower and towing capacity, but higher efficiency and instant torque
Environmental impact	Produce tailpipe emissions and contribute to air pollution and climate change	Produce zero tailpipe emissions and are a cleaner form of transportation
Brand and reputation	Wide variety of brands and reputations, some with strong track records for quality and innovation	Limited number of brands, but generally have strong track records for quality and innovation

When we look at the actual performance of gas cars and their electric counterpart we can see that BEVs are in reality in general much more powerful than gas cars.

Make/Model	Gas Car Horsepower	Comparable EV Horsepower
Audi A4	201 hp	Audi e-tron GT: 469 hp
BMW 3 Series	255 hp	BMW i4: 536 hp
Ford Mustang	310 hp	Ford Mustang Mach-E: 255-459 hp (varies by model)
Porsche 911	379 hp	Porsche Taycan: 402-750 hp (varies by model)
Tesla Model S	412-1020 hp (varies by model)	Tesla Model S: 412-1020 hp (varies by model)
Chevrolet Camaro	275-650 hp (varies by model)	Chevrolet Bolt EV: 200 hp

RANGE AND BATTERY CAPACITY

Range and battery capacity are important factors to consider when buying an electric car, as they can affect the car's overall usefulness and convenience.

Range is the distance that an electric car can travel on a single charge, and it is an important consideration for anyone who wants to use their car for longer trips or daily commuting. In general, the longer the range of an electric car, the more versatile it will be. A longer range means that the driver will be able to travel further without having to stop to charge the car, which can be more convenient and time-efficient.

Battery capacity is also an important consideration when buying an electric car, as it can affect the range and charging time of the car. The larger the battery capacity, the longer the range of the car and the longer the time it will take to charge.

In general, the ideal range and battery capacity will depend on the driver's individual needs and usage patterns. Someone who primarily uses their car for short trips around town may not need a car with a long range or large battery capacity, while someone who frequently travels long distances may prioritize a longer range and larger battery capacity.

Overall, when buying an electric car, it is important to consider both the range and battery capacity, as they are key factors in determining the usefulness and convenience of the vehicle.

CHARGING OPTIONS AND INFRASTRUCTURE

Electric vehicles (EVs) are becoming more and more popular as people become more concerned about the environment and the cost of gas. While EVs are a great way to reduce your carbon footprint and save money on gas, one of the biggest concerns for drivers is the availability of charging options and infrastructure. We'll take a look at the current state of EV charging options and infrastructure and what the future may hold.

Current State of EV Charging Options—Overview

Today, there are three main types of EV charging options:

- Level 1,
- Level 2, and
- DC fast charging.

Level 1 charging uses a standard 120-volt electrical outlet and can take up to 20 hours to fully charge an EV. Level 2 charging uses a 240-volt electrical circuit, similar to the circuit used for a clothes dryer, and can fully charge an EV in 4-8 hours. DC fast charging is the fastest option, using a high-powered charging station that can charge an EV to 80% in as little as 30 minutes.

The availability of charging options varies by location, with more charging stations being available in urban areas and along major highways. Public charging stations can be found at a variety of locations, including parking garages, shopping centers, and even some gas stations. Many EV owners also choose to install a home charging station for convenient charging at home.

Future of EV Charging Infrastructure

The future of EV charging infrastructure is looking bright, with many governments and companies investing in the expansion and improvement of charging options. For example, in the United States, the Biden administration has proposed a $174 billion investment in EVs and charging infrastructure, including the installation of 500,000 public charging stations by 2030.

Companies like Tesla and Volkswagen are also investing heavily in charging infrastructure, with Tesla building out its Supercharger network and Volkswagen investing in its Electrify America network. New charging technologies are also being developed, including wireless charging and ultra-fast charging, which could greatly improve the convenience and speed of charging.

One of the biggest challenges for the future of EV charging infrastructure is the need to balance the demand for charging with the availability of electricity. This will require new technologies and infrastructure to manage the supply and demand of electricity, as well as continued investment in renewable energy sources to power EVs.

Overall, the current state of EV charging options and infrastructure is improving, with more options available in more locations than ever before. The future looks even brighter, with continued investment in charging infrastructure and the development of new technologies to improve charging speed and convenience.

If you're considering purchasing an EV, it's important to research the charging options available in your area and plan for convenient and reliable charging. With the right planning and infrastructure, EVs can provide a clean and efficient mode of transportation that can help to reduce your carbon footprint and save you money on gas.

UNIQUE EV FEATURES

Battery electric vehicles (BEVs) and gas cars may look similar on the outside, but they are quite different in terms of their user features. Now, we'll take a look at the key user features of BEVs compared to gas cars.

Electrical Cabin Heating

BEVs have the ability to use electrical heating, while gas cars use a combustion engine to produce heat. This means that BEVs can run a heater when parked without running the engine, and use less energy to heat the cabin, which can save energy and improve efficiency. Some BEVs also have the ability to use heat pumps, which can further improve efficiency and reduce the energy needed for heating.

Electronic Features

BEVs often have advanced electronic features, including touch-screens, digital displays, and advanced driver assistance systems. These features can improve the driving experience and provide more information and control to the driver.

Entertainment Features

BEVs often have advanced entertainment features, including high-quality sound systems, streaming capabilities, and other options. This can provide a more enjoyable driving experience and make the vehicle more versatile for different uses.

Energy Recovery

BEVs have the ability to recover energy during braking, which can improve efficiency and reduce wear on the brakes. This feature is not available in gas cars, and it can save energy and money over time.

Charging Information

BEVs often have advanced charging information, including real-time charging status, charging station locations, and other details. This can help drivers plan their trips and make charging more convenient and efficient.

Navigation

BEVs often have advanced navigation features, including built-in maps, real-time traffic information, and other options. This can help drivers plan their trips more efficiently and find the most convenient charging stations along the way.

EVs are Smartphone on Wheels

People often refer to electric cars as a "smartphone on wheels" because of the significant technological advancements that have been incorporated into them. Like smartphones, electric cars are highly connected and can be controlled and monitored remotely through mobile apps. They are equipped with sophisticated features such as touch screens, voice commands, and advanced driver assistance systems that make them more convenient and easier to use. In addition, they often receive regular software updates that improve their performance, just like smartphones.

Moreover, electric cars are often seen as the next generation of automobiles that will transform the way we drive and interact with our vehicles, just as smartphones revolutionized the way we communicate and access information. They offer a glimpse into the future of transportation, with the potential to reduce carbon emissions and help create a cleaner, more sustainable world.

Overall, BEVs offer many advanced user features that are not available in gas cars. From electrical heating to advanced electronics, entertainment, energy recovery, and charging information, BEVs can provide a more efficient, enjoyable, and convenient driving experience. By understanding these user features, you can make an informed decision and choose the vehicle that is right for your needs and preferences.

EVs are Smartphones on Wheels

CHAPTER 5

Charging an Electric Car

In this chapter, we'll provide practical tips for charging an electric car. We'll explain the different types of charging stations and their associated charging times, as well as provide guidance on how to plan for longer trips.

Additionally, we'll address common concerns about charging, such as the availability of charging stations and the cost of charging, and provide real-world examples of electric car ownership to help readers understand what it's like to charge an electric car.

Charging is a critical part of owning an electric car, and understanding the different types of charging can help you make the most of your electric car.

NEW TO EV CHARGING?

For new electric vehicle (EV) owners, the learning curve for EV charging can be steep. While the overall process of charging an EV is straightforward, there are several things that new EV owners need to learn and adapt to.

One of the first things new EV owners need to comprehend is the different charging options available. As we know, there are three primary charging levels: Level 1, Level 2, and DC fast charging. Level 1 charging uses a standard household outlet and provides a slow charge rate of around 4-5 miles of range per hour. Level 2 charging requires a 220 V outlet and can provide a faster charge rate of approximately 20-30 miles of range per hour.

Level 1 Charging

Level 1 charging is the slowest and most basic form of charging. It uses a standard 120-volt electrical outlet and a special charging cord that comes with your electric car. Level 1 charging can take anywhere from 8 to 20 hours to fully charge a car, depending on the size of the battery.

While level 1 charging is the least convenient form of charging, it can be a good option for people who don't drive long distances or who have access to charging at work or other locations.

Level 2 Charging

Level 2 charging is a faster and more convenient form of charging. It uses a special charging station that is wired to a 220-volt electrical circuit, which is similar to the circuit used for a clothes dryer or electric oven.

Level 2 charging can fully charge an electric car in anywhere from 4 to 10 hours, depending on the size of the battery. Many electric car owners choose to install a level 2 charging station in their home, which provides the convenience of fast charging without the need to visit a public charging station.

For Level 2 charging, new EV owners need to install a 220 V charging outlet at their homes or find charging stations in public areas. Level 2 charging can provide a faster charge rate than Level 1, but it does require a specialized power outlet, which runs between 500$ and $1,000 to install at home.

DC Fast Charging

DC fast charging, also known as level 3 charging, is the fastest form of charging. It uses a high-powered charging station that can charge an electric car to 80% in as little as 30 minutes.

DC fast charging is primarily used for long-distance travel and is typically found at public charging stations along highways and major routes. While DC fast charging is more expensive than other forms of charging, it provides the convenience of fast charging on the go.

Once new EV owners understand the charging options available, they should familiarize themselves with their area's charging networks. Different charging networks may have other pricing models, subscription requirements, and access limitations, so it's essential to research and understand the options available.

New EV owners should also establish new charging habits. Unlike traditional gas-powered vehicles requiring refueling when the fuel gauge gets low, EV owners can plug in their vehicle anytime. However, to ensure that the car is always charged when needed, it's essential to establish a routine for charging the vehicle regularly. For example, some EV owners plug in their vehicles every night, while others charge their vehicles during the day at work.

Charging Speeds and Battery Management System

Every EV has a built-in AC/DC converter for charging from a wall charger that allows Level 1 and Level 2 charging. For faster charging, such a converter would be too big to fit into the car. This is why fast chargers already deliver DC for fast charging and offers the fastest speeds, up to 1,000 miles/hour. But it is only available at specific locations and can potentially degrade the battery's health over time if not managed properly by the car's electronic battery management system (BMS) which will ensure the battery will be charged based on its specefications. Below is an illustration of the resulting charging speed for DC and AC charging.

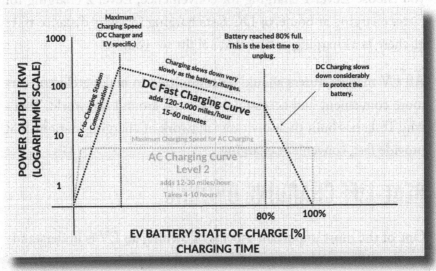

Illustration of AC and DC Charge Time and Delivered Charging Power

Finally, new EV owners should understand fast charging, its use cases, and its limitations. While fast charging can be convenient for long road trips, it can potentially degrade the battery's health over time if used excessively. Therefore, it's important to use fast charging sparingly and to stick to Level 1 and Level 2 charging for daily use.

The learning curve for new EV owners to learn about charging networks, new charging habits, and fast and slow charging can be challenging. However, with research and practice, new EV owners can quickly adapt and enjoy the benefits of owning an electric vehicle.

SUMMARY OF CHARGING TYPES

So there you have it, folks. Understanding the different types of charging is an important part of owning an electric car. Whether you choose Level 1 charging for convenience, Level 2 charging for faster charging at home, or DC fast charging for long-distance travel, there is a charging option that's right for you.

All EV manufacturers should be committed to making electric cars more convenient and accessible to people around the world. That's why Tesla has built their own vast network of charging stations that provide fast, convenient charging.

REAL-LIFE CHARGING OPTIONS

One of the most important aspects of owning an EV is understanding the different charging options available. In this section, we'll explore the three real-life charging options for EVs:

- fast charging,
- destination charging, and
- home charging.

As an EV owner you will very quickly learn to appreciate all three charging options. All of these three options have their pros and cons.

Fast Charging

Fast charging is the quickest way to charge your EV on the go. Fast charging stations can charge an EV up to 80% in as little as 20 minutes. These charging stations are usually located along major highways, in shopping centers, and other public places.

Most EVs can be charged at fast charging stations, but it's important to check if your car is compatible with the specific charging standard used by the station. Some popular fast charging standards include CHAdeMO, CCS, and Tesla Superchargers.

The two largest fast charging networks are currently *Electrify America* for CHAdeMo and CCS and the *Tesla Supercharger* network proviging currently the Tesla Connector.

Destination Charging

Destination charging refers to charging your EV at a specific destination, such as a hotel, restaurant, or mall. These charging stations are usually Level 2 chargers and can provide a few miles per hour to your EV's battery while you're out and about.

Many hotels and other businesses are starting to offer destination charging as a perk for their customers, making it even easier for EV owners to travel longer distances.

While it's true that destination chargers are perfect for places where you plan to stay for a while, like hotels or resorts, charging up at a grocery store like Safeway may not be the best idea. Let's face it, you'll probably only be able to add a few miles to your car's range while you're picking out your favorite snacks and groceries. So, unless you're planning on driving your EV from aisle to aisle (which would be pretty cool, actually), it's not going to add much value to your journey. So, why not save your charging for a more exciting destination and just enjoy your shopping trip without any extra stops at a charger? After all, grocery shopping can be stressful enough without worrying about your EV's battery life!

Home Charging

Home charging is the most convenient and cost-effective way to charge your EV.

All you need is a dedicated charging station installed in your garage or driveway, which can be done by a certified electrician. Most EVs come at least with a Level 1 charging cord and adapter that can be plugged into a regular household outlet, but this charging method is slow and not recommended for daily use.

A Level 2 charging adapter is the best option for home charging, as it can charge an EV up to six times faster than a Level 1 charger. Depending on the EV and the charging station, it can take anywhere from a few hours to overnight to fully charge your car at home.

Installation Requirements and Instructions

To install a Level 2 home charging station, you will need a dedicated 220- or 240-volt electrical circuit, a compatible charging station, and a licensed electrician to install the circuit and outlet. The cost of installation can vary depending on the location and complexity of the installation, but it is generally less expensive than installing a gas pump in your home.

The installation of an EV home charger is similar in some ways to the installation of a dryer outlet, but there are also some key differences to be aware of.

In terms of similarities, both the EV charger and dryer outlet require a dedicated 220V circuit with the appropriate amperage and wiring size to handle the load. Both also require a suitable outlet or receptacle to plug in the device.

However, there are some important differences to note. For example, the EV charger will likely require a higher amperage circuit than the dryer outlet, typically ranging from 30 to 60 amps depending on the specific charger and vehicle. This means that the wiring and circuit breaker must be appropriately sized to accommodate the higher load.

Additionally, the installation of an EV charger may require more planning and preparation than a dryer outlet. Depending on the specific installation site and the requirements of the charger, it may be necessary to run new wiring from the main electrical panel to the location of the charger, or to install a subpanel or load center to handle the additional circuits. This can involve more extensive electrical work and may require the services of a licensed electrician.

Overall, while there are some similarities between the installation of an EV charger and a dryer outlet, the EV charger typically requires a more robust electrical setup and may involve more complex installation procedures. It is important to carefully review the manufacturer's installation instructions and consult with a qualified electrician to ensure that the installation is done safely and properly.

You can install an outlet box as illustrated below or a wall outlet. Here is a picture of an outlet box and a plug that will connect to your EV charger.

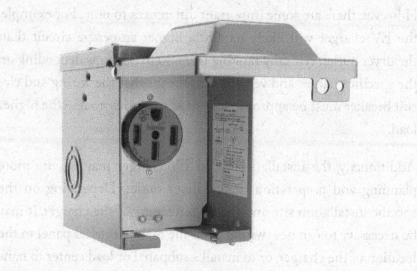

Nema 14–50 220 Volt Outlet Box.

The Nema 14–50 220 Volt Plug is attached to your EV charger adapter, which comes with the purchase of your EV.

Charging when living in an Appartment

If you live in an apartment or other multi-unit building and own an electric car, charging at home might be a challenge. But there are several options available for charging at home.

- Use a public charging station: If your building management is unable or unwilling to install charging infrastructure, you can look for public charging stations in your area. While not as convenient as charging at home, this can be a viable option for apartment-dwellers who have access to public charging stations nearby.
- Consider a portable charging solution: There are several portable EV charging solutions (e.g. SparkCharge) on the market, which can be a good option for apartment-dwellers who don't have access to a dedicated charging station. These can be plugged into a standard electrical outlet and provide a slow but steady charge to your EV.
- Share a charging station with a neighbor: If you have a neighbor who also owns an EV, you could consider sharing the cost of installing a dedicated charging station in your building's parking area.
- Join a shared charging network: Some cities have shared charging networks, which allow EV owners to share access to a dedicated charging station in a common parking area.
- Work with your building management: Start by talking to your building management or landlord about your interest in charging your EV at home. In some cases, they may be willing to install charging infrastructure or allow you to do so at your own expense. On the next page is a template for a letter to your landlord or building management:

[Your Name]
[Your Address]
[City, State ZIP Code]
[Date]

[Apartment Complex Name]
[Address]
[City, State ZIP Code]

Dear [Building Management or Landlord],

I hope this letter finds you well. I am writing to express my strong interest in the installation of overnight electric vehicle (EV) charging stations in our apartment complex. As an EV owner, I am deeply committed to reducing my carbon footprint and contributing to a cleaner and more sustainable environment. However, one of the biggest challenges I face is finding convenient and accessible places to charge my vehicle.

I strongly believe that the installation of overnight EV charging stations in our apartment complex would be a significant step towards a greener future. By providing residents with the necessary infrastructure to charge their EVs, you will not only support those who have made the switch to electric but also help encourage more people to make the transition. Additionally, offering EV charging stations would be a valuable amenity for the complex, attracting environmentally conscious tenants and adding to the overall value of the property.

I understand that the installation of overnight EV charging stations is a significant investment. However, there are many programs and incentives available for businesses and property owners looking to install EV charging stations. These programs can significantly reduce the costs associated with installation, making it an attractive and affordable option.

I would be happy to discuss this matter further with you and provide additional information about the benefits and potential incentives associated with installing overnight EV charging stations. Thank you for your time and consideration, and I look forward to hearing from you.

Sincerely,

[Your Name]

Overall, there are several options available for apartment-dwellers who want to charge their EV at home. While some of these may require some extra effort or expense, they can ultimately make EV ownership more accessible and convenient for everyone.

Charging Cost at your Private Home

The cost of charging your BEV at home will depend on your electricity rates and the efficiency of your vehicle. However, in general, the cost of charging a BEV at home is much less than the cost of fueling a gas car.

Let's say you like to calculate the cost of charging your car's 75 kWh battery at a rate of 10 cents per kWh, you can use the following formula:

Cost = kWh x Cost per kWh

So, for a 75 kWh battery:

Cost = 75 kWh x $0.10/kWh

Cost = $7.50

Therefore, it would cost $7.50 at home to fully charge your car's 75 kWh battery at a rate of 10 cents per kWh. However, please note that you typically do not charge your EV from 0-100%. A typical charging range would be between 20% and 80% to keep your battery in good health. So, a full charge would be 60% (100%-20%-20%) of $7.50, which is $4.50.

In general, charging an EV is not likely to use more energy than running a cloth dryer. According to the US Department of Energy, the average home clothes dryer uses about 3.3 kilowatt-hours (kWh) of electricity per cycle. In contrast, a typical EV battery has a capacity of around 50-100 kWh, meaning that even a full charge would use less energy than running a clothes dryer.

It is also worth noting that the energy used by an EV during charging can be offset by the use of renewable energy sources such as solar or wind power. Additionally, many EV owners take advantage of time-of-use rates, charging their vehicles during off-peak hours when electricity is less expensive.

Overall, while the energy usage of both an EV and a clothes dryer can vary, it is unlikely that charging an EV would use more energy than running a clothes dryer. You can also take advantage of time-of-use rates and other incentives to further reduce the cost of charging at home.

Benefits of Home Charging

Home charging offers several benefits for BEV owners, including convenience, reliability, and cost savings. With a home charging station, you can charge your vehicle overnight or during off-peak hours, which can help you avoid the hassle of finding a public charging station. You also have the peace of mind of knowing that your vehicle will always be charged and ready to go when you need it.

Best Practices for Home Charging

To make the most of home charging, it's important to follow some best practices, including:

- Install a charging station that is compatible with your vehicle
- Use a licensed electrician for installation
- Follow the manufacturer's instructions for charging
- Plan your charging around your driving needs and electricity rates

- Monitor your vehicle's battery health to ensure optimal performance

Overall, home charging is a convenient, reliable, and cost-effective way to charge your BEV. By understanding the types of home charging, installation requirements, charging cost, benefits, and best practices, you can make the most of this convenient option and enjoy the benefits of driving a BEV.

PUBLIC CHARGING

While home charging is a convenient option for many BEV owners, public charging is an essential option for longer trips and when charging at home is not possible or on longer trips. In this section, we'll take a look at public charging of BEVs and what you need to know to make the most of this option.

Types of Public Charging

There are three main types of public charging for BEVs:

- Level 2,
- DC fast charging, and
- Tesla Supercharging.

Level 2 charging uses a 240-volt electrical circuit and can fully charge an EV in 4-8 hours. DC fast charging is the fastest option, using a high-powered charging station that can charge an EV to 80% in as little as 30 minutes. Tesla Supercharging is a proprietary charging network that is today mostly only available to Tesla owners.

Charging Networks

There are several charging networks available for public charging, including ChargePoint, EVgo, Electrify America, and Tesla Supercharging. Each network has its own pricing, access, and availability, so it's important to research the networks in your area and choose the one that best fits your needs.

CHARGING PLUGS AND ADAPTERS

Unfortunately, there is still a lack of standardization in the electric vehicle charging industry, particularly in terms of charging plugs and protocols. In a 2019 interview, Elon Musk said, "*It's crazy that we don't have a standard worldwide for charging. We're going to have to work towards something like that.*" He has even suggested that Tesla might be willing to share its charging technology with other automakers to help move the industry towards a more unified standard, which he did in late 2022. On the following page, I included a table that lists some of the major electric vehicle (EV) fast-charging networks, along with the number of charge stations, reliability, and availability information.

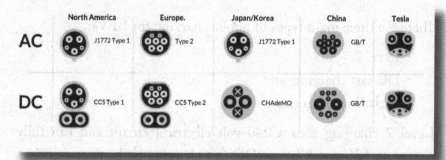

Worldwide EV Charger Standards for AC and DC charging

In the USA are only two fast charging connectors relevant, the CCS and the Tesla connectors. I left out the CHAdeMo connector because of a declining usage in the market.

Fast and Level 2 Charging Standards

CCS Connector
(Combined Charging System)

Used by all other EVs

Tesla Connector

Used only for Tesla EVs

Currently, an adapter is available to connect a Tesla connector to a CCS plug. Tesla is now working on making Tesla chargers also available to EVs using a CCS connector.

CCS to Tesla Adapter

Tesla owners can also use an adapter to charge at Level 2 chargers for EVs using the CCS standard for Level 2 chargning, which is the J1772 connector.

Level 2 (j1772) to Tesla Adapter

My Personal Experience with Charghing Networks

When I first got my hands on a Nissan Leaf, I was thrilled with the idea of driving a car that didn't rely on dirty gasoline. But as I started exploring the open road, I quickly realized the importance of charging away from home if I wanted to use my EV for more than just grocery runs.

Nissan dealerships were a great start for free fast-charging, but the proprietary charging plug, called CHAdeMO, left me in a bit of a bind. Finding non-Nissan charging stations was tough, and planning detours to reach charging stations took more effort than I wanted to put in. Plus, other public charging networks like Electrify America and Blink Charging just weren't as reliable as I had hoped. Nothing is worse than being stranded with a dead battery.

That's when I made the leap to a Tesla Model S in 2022, and let me tell you, the Tesla Supercharger network blew me away. Tesla has made a huge effort to create the largest and most reliable charging network in the world, and the user experience and practicality of using the Tesla supercharging network surpasses other charging networks by far. It's a game changer, folks!

Now, even non-Tesla car dealerships are offering free fast-charging at Electrify America with the purchase of a new EV, which is great news for the EV community. However, with the increased demand for public charging, some CCS charging networks are struggling to keep up, which can leave many EV drivers stranded. So, make sure you know what to expect when it comes to fast charging with your electric vehicle.

Cost of Public Charging

The cost of public charging can vary depending on the charging network, location, and type of charging. Some networks offer pay-as-you-go pricing, while others offer subscription plans or per-kilowatt-hour pricing. In general, the cost of public charging is three to four times higher than the cost of home charging, but it can be a convenient option for longer trips and when charging at home is not possible.

Availability of Public Charging

The availability of public charging varies by location, with more charging stations being available in urban areas and along major highways. Public charging stations can be found at a variety of locations, including parking garages, shopping centers, and even some gas stations. It's important to plan your route and charging stops in advance to ensure that you have access to charging stations along the way.

Best Practices for Public Charging

To make the most of public charging, it's important to follow some best practices, including:

- Research the charging networks and stations in your area
- Plan your route and charging stops in advance
- Monitor your vehicle's battery status and charging progress
- Be mindful of other EV drivers and share charging stations when possible

Overall, public charging is an essential option for BEV owners, providing convenient and reliable charging for longer trips and when charging at home is not possible. By understanding the types of public charging, charging networks, cost, availability, and best practices, you can make the most of this option and enjoy the benefits of driving a BEV.

EVS, SOFTWARE AND MOBILE APPS

Most traditional car companies struggle with the switch from a pure mechanical manufacturers to a software company. The Tesla mobile app is maybe the most reliable app that allows Tesla owners to monitor and control their cars remotely. The app provides access to a range of features, including remote climate control, charging information, location tracking, and more. In addition, the app is regularly updated with new features and functionality.

One of the most exciting developments for the Tesla app is its potential use for robotaxi services. Tesla CEO Elon Musk has stated that the company plans to use the app as a platform for a fully autonomous ride-hailing service. This service, dubbed the "Tesla Network," would allow Tesla owners to add their cars to the fleet of self-driving robotaxis, earning money from the service while their car is not in use. The app would be used to request rides, track vehicle location and availability, and process payments.

Currently, the Tesla app also offers a "Smart Summon" feature, which allows Tesla owners to remotely summon their car from a parking space to their location using the app. Owners can share the access to the vehicle with other smarphone users. This feature relies on the car's advanced autopilot system and requires a clear line of sight to the vehicle.

Overall, the Tesla app is a crucial tool for any Tesla owner and offers a glimpse into the potential future of transportation with the advent of self-driving cars and robotaxis. As Tesla continues to innovate and develop new features for the app, it is likely to play an even more significant role in the future of the automotive industry.

The Tesla App

Here is a table that shows some of the major EV fast charging networks and their reliability, number of charger ports nationwide, and availability.

Fast-Charging Network	Number of Charge Stations	Reliability	Availability
Tesla Supercharger	25,000+ (worldwide)	High	Exclusive to Tesla vehicles as of 2023
Electrify America	500+ (in the US)	High	Open to all EVs
ChargePoint	131,000+ (worldwide)	High	Open to all EVs
EVgo	800+ (in the US)	High	Open to all EVs
Ionity	400+ (in Europe)	High	Open to all EVs
Greenlots	50,000+ (worldwide)	High	Open to all EVs
Blink Charging	4,000+ (in the US)	Moderate	Open to all EVs
Enel X	10,000+ (worldwide)	High	Open to all EVs
Shell Recharge	300+ (in Europe)	High	Open to all EVs
BP Chargemaster	7,000+ (in the UK)	High	Open to all EVs

The provided table on EV fast-charging networks is based on a combination of sources, including official websites, news articles, industry reports, and personal experience. However, the information may change over time as new networks emerge and existing ones expand or modify their offerings. It's also important to note that reliability and availability may vary depending on location and specific charging stations. There are many other networks operating worldwide, with new ones emerging as the demand for EVs and fast charging infrastructure grows.

CHARGING ETIQUETTE

As electric vehicles (EVs) become more popular, so too does the need for fast charging stations to power them up quickly. But just as there are rules of the road for driving, there are also guidelines for EV fast charging etiquette that every EV driver should know.

First and foremost, it's important to be aware of the charging station's availability. If there is a line of EVs waiting to charge, be considerate and avoid hogging the charger for longer than necessary. Most charging stations have a time limit, so once your EV is charged, be sure to move it out of the way for the next driver.

Additionally, it's important to be aware of the charging rate. EV charging stations have different charging rates, so be sure to read the instructions before plugging in. If you notice that your EV is charging faster than the rate specified by the charging station, unplug and move to a station with a higher charging rate. This will help prevent long wait times for other EV drivers.

It's also important to be mindful of EV charging station parking. EV charging stations are often located in high traffic areas, so be sure to park your EV in the designated charging spot. Avoid parking your EV in a charging spot if you are not actively charging, as this can prevent other EV drivers from accessing the charger. And if the charging station is located in a private parking lot, be sure to check if there are any specific parking rules or fees.

Finally, it's important to maintain good charging habits. Always be sure to charge your EV to a sufficient level for your next trip, and avoid leaving your EV charging for an extended period of time if it is already fully charged. This will help ensure that the charging station is available for other EV drivers who need it.

> *By following these guidelines, you can help promote a positive charging experience for all EV drivers. Remember, being courteous and considerate goes a long way towards creating a positive EV driving community.*

The below diagram gives you a quick overview of the three main charging types. Important to note is that each type is important for the practial use of your EV. An example of a not very effective use of a Level 2 charging application are Level 2 chargers at grocery stores. Typically, these chargers only add a few miles to the car while shopping, which will not be practial when the EV owner lives not close to the store. Level 2 chargers at stores only make sense as emergency chargers to enable stranded EV drivers to reach a closeby destination.

Level 1 Trickle Charging	**Level 2** Destination/Home Charging	**DC Fast Charge** Superchargers/Fast Chargers
VOLTAGE	**VOLTAGE**	**VOLTAGE**
120 V 1-Phase AC	220 V 2-Phase AC	280–480 V DC
AMPS	**AMPS**	**AMPS**
12 to 16 Amps	12–80 Amps (Typ 32 Amps)	up to 125 Amps
CHARGING LOADS	**CHARGING LOADS**	**CHARGING LOADS**
1.4 to 1.9 kW	2.5 to 19.2 kW (Typ 7 KW)	50 kW to 250 kW
CHARGING TIME	**CHARGING TIME**	**CHARGING TIME**
3-5 miles/hour	10-30 miles/hour	up to 250 miles/hour
PRICE PER MILE	**PRICE PER MILE**	**PRICE PER MILE**
2 cents - 6 cents/mile	2 cents - 6 cents/mile	12 cents - 25 cents/mile
LOCATION	**LOCATION**	**LOCATION**
Typically Home only	Public and Home	Public only
WHEN	**WHEN**	**WHEN**
Emergency only	Daily at Home or Destination	Only during long trips

Charging Types: Overview Diagram

CHAPTER 6

Maintaining an Electric Car

In this chapter, we'll discuss how to maintain an electric car, including regular maintenance tasks such as tire rotations and brake inspections.

Maintaining an electric car (EV) is a little different from maintaining a traditional gasoline-powered car, but it's just as important to keep up with regular maintenance to keep your car running smoothly and efficiently. Here are some tips for maintaining your EV:

Follow the manufacturer's recommended maintenance schedule: Just like with a gas car, your EV's manufacturer will provide a recommended maintenance schedule in the owner's manual. This schedule will include regular maintenance tasks like tire rotations, brake checks, and battery checks. Following this schedule will help keep your EV in good working order and prevent any major issues from arising.

Keep the battery charged: Keeping the battery charged is essential to maintaining the health of your EV. It's important to charge your EV regularly and not let the battery level get too low. Be sure to use a high-quality charging cable and charger, and avoid using aftermarket chargers or cables that could damage the battery.

Monitor battery health: While EV batteries are designed to be durable and long-lasting, it's still important to monitor the health of your battery over time. Check the battery's state of health regularly, and look for signs of degradation or other issues. If you notice any problems, take your EV to a qualified service center for a check-up.

Check the tires: Just like with any car, it's important to keep an eye on the condition of your EV's tires. Check the tire pressure regularly and look for signs of wear or damage. Rotate your tires as recommended by the manufacturer to ensure even wear and prolong the life of the tires.

Keep up with software updates: Many EV manufacturers release regular software updates for their vehicles, which can help improve performance and fix any bugs or issues. Be sure to keep up with these updates and install them as recommended by the manufacturer.

Find a qualified service center: Finally, it's important to find a qualified service center that's familiar with EVs and can provide the specialized maintenance and repair services that your car needs. Look for a service center that's been certified by the EV manufacturer and has experience working with EVs.

By following these tips and keeping up with regular maintenance, you can help ensure that your EV is always in top working order and ready to take you where you need to go. With proper care and attention, your EV can provide years of reliable and sustainable transportation.

REGULAR MAINTENANCE

The maintenance requirements for electric vehicles (EVs) are generally less frequent and less intensive than those of traditional gas-powered vehicles. While the specifics of a maintenance schedule can vary depending on the make and model of the EV, there are some common tasks that should be performed regularly:

Tire rotation: Just like with gas-powered cars, it is recommended to rotate your EV's tires every 5,000-7,500 miles to ensure even wear.

Brake system check: EVs use regenerative braking to slow the car down, which can reduce the wear and tear on the brakes. However, it is still important to have the brakes checked regularly to ensure they are functioning properly.

Battery inspection: Most EVs have a built-in battery management system that monitors the health of the battery. It is recommended to have the battery inspected periodically to ensure it is functioning properly and to check for signs of degradation.

Cabin air filter replacement: The cabin air filter should be replaced every 15,000-30,000 miles, or more frequently if you frequently drive in dusty or polluted environments.

Coolant check: Some EVs have a coolant system for the battery and/or the motor. It is important to have the coolant levels checked and topped off as needed.

It is also recommended to follow the manufacturer's guidelines for regular service and inspection, which can vary depending on the specific make and model of the EV. However, in general, EVs require less frequent maintenance than traditional gas-powered cars, which can save time and money in the long run.

BATTERY MAINTENANCE

Proper battery maintenance is an important aspect of owning an electric vehicle (EV). While EV batteries are designed to be durable and long-lasting, they do require some maintenance to ensure optimal performance and extend the life of the battery.

Here are some tips for maintaining your EV battery:

- **Keep the battery charged:** One of the most important things you can do to maintain your EV battery is to keep it charged. Make sure to charge your battery regularly and avoid letting it drain completely. This will help ensure that the battery stays healthy and has a long life.

- **Avoid extreme temperatures:** Extreme temperatures, both hot and cold, can be harmful to your EV battery. Try to park your vehicle in a garage or shaded area to protect it from direct sunlight and extreme heat. Similarly, avoid exposing your battery to extreme cold by parking your vehicle in a heated garage or using a battery warmer in cold weather.

- **Monitor battery health:** It's important to monitor the health of your EV battery over time. Check the battery's state of health regularly and look for signs of degradation or other issues. If you notice any problems, take your EV to a qualified service center for a check-up.

- **Use the right charging equipment:** Using the right charging equipment is essential for maintaining your EV battery. Use a high-quality charging cable and charger, and avoid using aftermarket chargers or cables that could damage the battery.

- **Consider battery replacement:** While EV batteries are designed to last a long time, they will eventually need to be replaced. When it's time to replace your battery, be sure to work with a qualified service center to ensure that the replacement battery is of the right quality and is installed correctly.

In general, by following these tips and staying on top of regular maintenance, you can help ensure that your EV battery stays healthy and performs at its best. With proper care and attention, your EV battery can provide years of reliable and sustainable transportation.

BATTERY DEGRADATION

Electric vehicle batteries are a critical component of an EV's powertrain, providing the energy needed to propel the vehicle and keep its various systems running. However, a battery does not last forever. The main two reasons why a battery becomes unusable are: *functional failure* (e.g. cell failure) and *capacity loss*. Capacity loss happens over time, and even the best EV batteries will gradually lose capacity due to a variety of factors. Functional failures can happen at any time during its use, even when brand new.

Functional Battery Failures

For most EV vehicles, a battery failure is typically defined as a malfunction or defect that results in the battery being unable to perform its intended function. This can include issues such as a complete loss of power, the inability to hold a charge, or any other problem that renders the battery unusable or significantly impairs its performance. If such a failure occurs within the 8-year warranty period, most EV manufacturers will typically repair or replace the battery under their warranty policy.

Capacity Loss

In EVs, battery capacity loss is defined as a gradual decrease in the amount of charge that the battery can hold over time. This can occur as a result of a variety of factors, including usage patterns, environmental conditions, and natural wear and tear. While battery capacity loss is an inevitable occurrence for all batteries, EV batteries are designed to retain a high level of performance for a prolonged period. If the capacity loss falls below a certain level during the 8-year warranty period, the car company will typically repair or replace the battery under their warranty policy. However, a certain degree of capacity loss over time is normal and is not typically considered a warranty issue.

One of the primary factors that can contribute to battery degradation is temperature. High temperatures can accelerate the rate at which battery cells degrade, reducing their overall capacity and ability to hold a charge. This is why it's important to avoid exposing your EV to extreme heat, and to park in the shade or a covered area whenever possible.

Another factor that can contribute to battery degradation is the depth of discharge. Battery cells are designed to operate within a certain range of charge levels, and allowing the battery to discharge too deeply can accelerate degradation. This is why it's important to avoid letting your EV's battery charge level drop too low, and to recharge it before it gets too low.

Charging speed can also impact battery degradation, as fast charging can generate more heat and contribute to greater capacity loss over time. It's generally recommended to avoid fast charging whenever possible, and to use a slower charging rate for day-to-day charging needs.

Over time, all batteries will naturally degrade due to the gradual chemical changes that occur within the cells. However, the rate of degradation can be affected by a variety of factors, including the battery chemistry, the quality of the manufacturing process, and the way the battery is used and maintained over time.

Fortunately, most EV batteries are designed to last for more than eight years, and many come with long-term warranties that provide additional peace of mind for owners. By following best practices for EV battery maintenance, monitoring battery health regularly, and seeking professional assistance as needed, EV owners can maximize the life of their battery and get the most out of their electric vehicle.

Temperature-Related Battery Degradation

One of the primary factors contributing to battery degradation is temperature. Let's explore the impact of temperature on EV battery degradation, including the effects of hot and cold temperatures, and provide recommendations for optimizing battery life.

How Temperature Affects EV Battery Degradation

Both high and low temperatures can lead to a decrease in battery capacity and performance. The following sections provide an in-depth analysis of the effects of temperature on battery degradation.

High Temperature Effects

Extreme heat can accelerate battery degradation in electric vehicles. The primary reasons for this acceleration are:

- **Increased internal resistance:** As temperature rises, the internal resistance of the battery increases, leading to a decrease in efficiency and an increase in heat generation during charging and discharging. This heat exacerbates degradation and can lead to a vicious cycle of heat buildup and degradation.

- **Electrolyte breakdown:** High temperatures can cause the electrolyte in the battery to break down, resulting in the formation of gas and other byproducts. These byproducts can lead to further degradation and reduced battery capacity.
- **Accelerated aging:** Elevated temperatures can also cause accelerated aging of battery components, such as the separator and the electrodes, leading to a reduction in overall battery life.

Low Temperature Effects

Cold temperatures can also negatively impact EV battery performance and degradation. The primary reasons for this include:

- **Reduced capacity:** At low temperatures, the electrolyte's viscosity increases, which reduces the battery's ability to deliver power. This results in a temporary decrease in battery capacity.
- **Increased internal resistance:** As with high temperatures, low temperatures can also increase the battery's internal resistance, leading to reduced efficiency and performance.
- **Longer charging times:** Cold temperatures slow down the chemical reactions within the battery, resulting in longer charging times.
- **Lithium plating:** In extreme cold, lithium ions can be deposited onto the anode as a solid metallic lithium layer, known as lithium plating. This process can cause permanent capacity loss and increase the risk of short-circuiting.

Strategies for Minimizing Temperature-Related Degradation

To mitigate the effects of temperature on battery degradation, the following strategies can be employed:

- **Thermal management systems:** Most modern EVs come equipped with thermal management systems that help maintain optimal battery temperatures. These systems use either air or liquid cooling to regulate the battery's temperature, improving performance and extending battery life.

- **Smart charging:** Charging your EV during cooler periods of the day or avoiding charging immediately after heavy use can help minimize heat buildup in the battery, reducing degradation.

- **Park in the shade:** Whenever possible, park your EV in a shaded area or use a sunshade to protect the battery from direct sunlight and high temperatures.

- **Pre-conditioning:** Many EVs offer the option to precondition the battery before use. By warming or cooling the battery to its optimal temperature range, you can improve performance and reduce the impact of temperature-related degradation.

Understanding the effects of temperature on EV battery degradation is essential for prolonging the life and performance of electric vehicles. By taking preventative measures and properly maintaining your EV, you can minimize the impact of temperature-related degradation.

Remaining Battery Life Estimation Algorithm

You might wonder if there is a formular to calculate battery degradation for your vehicle. Based on my research, the answer is no. However, I developed a formula emprically that comes pretty close to the actual degradation curve. The forumula is based on a formula for a parabola with an opening at the top. The formula is as follows:

$$y = kx^2 - cx + 100$$

Whereas:

y = remaining battery capacity in [%] (degradation=100-y)

k = degradation constant (0.0003075, same for each vehicle)

c = car model coefficient (different for each vehicle model)

x = number of months/years

While k is always the same value of 0.0003075, c is vehicle specific. Here are some approximate empirically determined examples for c:

Tesla Model S, c = 0.025

Nissan Leaf, c = 0.06

Ford Mustang Mach-E, c = 0.05

The lower c, the less battery degradation, and the longer the battery will keep its capacity.

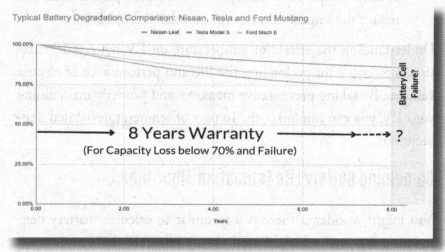

Data Source: geotab.com/fleet-management-solutions/ev-battery-degradation-tool

After the manufacturer's 8-year warranty period has ended, there is a good chance that the battery will continue to function for a long time, and the rate of capacity loss may even decrease. However, as the battery ages, there is an increased likelihood that one or more cells inside the battery casing may fail and cause an electrical short. Fortunately, there are companies that specialize in repairing damaged cells, which can effectively bring the battery back to life.

CHARGING HABITS AFFECT DEGRADATION

One of the key factors in battery degradation is how often and how quickly an EV is charged. Over time, repeated fast charging can cause the battery to degrade faster. This is why many experts recommend using slower, Level 2 charging whenever possible, and reserving fast charging for emergencies or when you're in a hurry.

But another, often overlooked factor to consider is how empty you let your battery get before charging, and how much your charge your battery each time. Certain charging habits can accelerate this degradation, while others can help to prolong battery life.

One common myth is that you should always charge your EV to 100% and avoid letting the battery drop below 20%. While this may have been true in the early days of EVs, modern battery management systems have made this less of an issue. In fact, charging to 100% on a regular basis can actually cause more wear and tear on the battery, and may lead to faster degradation over time. Similarly, constantly draining the battery to near-empty levels can also be detrimental to battery health.

So, what's the solution? Experts recommend aiming for a "sweet spot" of sorts when it comes to charging, which might be when you aim to keep your battery level between 25-75%. This allows for a healthy balance between usable range and battery longevity when using a slower charging method, such as a Level 2 charger, because it is less stressful on the battery than fast charging at a DC fast charger.

Research performed by the IEEE[1] revealed degredation curves for different charging habits, which show that the best battery retention is achieved by keeping the charge always between 65% and 75%.

Of course, this is not a realistic scenario for any EV owner. A good and realistic comprimise could be between 25-75% or 25-85% range. But every EV and battery is different, and it's always a good idea to consult your owner's manual or speak with a qualified technician to determine the best charging habits for your specific vehicle. With a little TLC, however, your EV battery can go the distance and provide reliable performance for years to come.

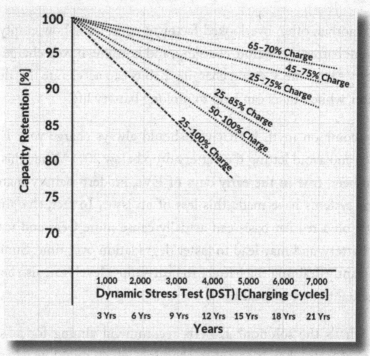

Diagram based on research performed by the IEEE: Modeling of Lithium-Ion Battery Degradation for Cell Life Assessment.

---

1   https://www.researchgate.net/publication/303890624_Modeling_of_Lithium-Ion_Battery_Degradation_for_Cell_Life_Assessment

NEW BATTERY TYPES

New battery developments, like Tesla's new 4680 battery technology, can revolutionize the EV industry with increased energy density, greater efficiency, and a streamlined design that may eventually eliminate the need for thousands of individual battery cells.

By introducing new batteries, manufacturers might update their recommended charging habits. Unlike previous recommendations to keep battery levels between 20-80%, they might suggest charging to 90% regularly for optimal performance and longevity. It's important to note that individual charging habits may vary based on vehicle use and climate conditions.

BATTERY REPLACEMENT AND REPAIR

When the electric vehicle owner decides to replace the battery, the old battery may be repurposed or recycled, depending on its condition and the policies of the manufacturer.

One possible use for old EV batteries is repurposing them for stationary energy storage applications, such as in homes, businesses, or even grid-scale energy storage. While the battery may no longer be suitable for an EV, it may still have a significant amount of usable capacity, which other companies can harness for different applications.

Another option for old EV batteries is to recycle them. EV batteries are made up of various materials, including metals like lithium, cobalt, and nickel, which can be recovered and used to create new batteries or other products. Therefore, recycling old batteries is essential to reducing the environmental impact of EVs and ensuring that the materials used in battery production are reused as much as possible.

Other factors that can impact the lifespan of an EV battery include the number of charging cycles, the charging speed, the temperature of the battery, and the overall maintenance and care of the battery. In general, most EV batteries are designed to last for several years, with many manufacturers offering warranties of 8-10 years or more.

When it's time to replace an EV battery, it's important to work with a qualified service center to ensure that the replacement battery is of the right quality and is installed correctly. By repurposing or recycling old EV batteries and properly maintaining and replacing batteries over time, we can ensure that EVs continue to provide sustainable and reliable transportation for years to come.

COMMON PROBLEMS AND REPAIRS WITH EVS

While electric vehicles (EVs) generally require less maintenance and repairs than traditional gasoline-powered cars, they can still experience some common problems and require repairs from time to time. Here are some of the most common problems and repairs for EVs:

Battery degradation: Over time, EV batteries can lose some of their capacity and performance, which can lead to reduced driving range and slower charging times. In some cases, the battery may need to be replaced, which can be expensive.

Charging issues: EVs rely on a complex charging system, which can sometimes experience issues with charging speed, compatibility with different chargers, or problems with the charging cable or port.

Electric motor issues: While EV motors are generally reliable and require little maintenance, they can sometimes experience issues with overheating or other performance problems that require repairs.

Brake issues: EVs use regenerative braking, which can reduce wear and tear on the brake pads, but they can still experience issues with the brake system that require repairs.

Electrical system issues: EVs rely on a complex electrical system to power the vehicle, including the battery, charging system, and motor. Problems with the electrical system can cause a variety of issues, including reduced performance, charging issues, and other problems.

Software issues: Like all modern vehicles, EVs rely on a complex software system to control various functions and features. Software issues can cause a variety of problems, including reduced performance, charging issues, and other issues.

In general, the key to preventing and addressing common problems and repairs for EVs is to stay on top of regular maintenance and address any issues promptly. By following the manufacturer's recommended maintenance schedule and working with a qualified service center, you can help ensure that your EV stays in top working order and provides reliable and sustainable transportation for years to come.

FINDING A QUALIFIED TECHNICIAN

Most car repair companies may not be an ideal choice for electric vehicles (EVs) because EVs have different components and systems than traditional gasoline-powered cars, requiring specialized knowledge and training to properly diagnose and repair.

For example, EVs have complex battery systems that require specialized knowledge to diagnose and repair. EVs also have regenerative braking systems, which require a different approach to brake maintenance and repair than traditional brake systems. Additionally, EVs have unique electrical systems, which require specialized training and equipment to diagnose and repair electrical issues.

Many traditional car repair companies may not have the specialized knowledge or training necessary to properly diagnose and repair EVs, which can lead to misdiagnoses, ineffective repairs, or even damage to the vehicle. This is why it's important to work with a qualified service center that has experience with EVs and is equipped with the specialized knowledge, tools, and equipment necessary to properly maintain and repair these vehicles.

In addition, traditional car repair companies may not have access to the specialized parts and components that are required for EVs, which can result in longer repair times or the use of inferior replacement parts.

While many traditional car repair companies may be able to handle some basic maintenance and repairs for EVs, it's important to work with a qualified service center that specializes in EVs and has the expertise, tools, and resources necessary to properly diagnose and repair these complex vehicles.

GRUBER MOTORS

Gruber Motors (https://grubermotors.com) is based in Phoenix, Arizona, and specializes in servicing and repairing Tesla electric vehicles (EVs). The company was founded by Pete Gruber. After Pete worked at Digital Equipment Corporation as a consulting engineer, he founded Gruber Motors, which offers a wide range of services for Tesla owners, including routine maintenance, battery replacement, and repairs for a variety of issues. The company has developed a reputation for its expertise and quality work, and is often recommended by Tesla owners and enthusiasts.

One of Gruber Motors' signature services is its battery replacement program, which offers customers the ability to replace their Tesla battery with a new or refurbished battery for a fraction of the cost of a new Tesla. A short phone call with Gruber Motors revealed that the cost would be much less that installing a new battery. The company has developed a proprietary process for refurbishing Tesla batteries, which allows them to offer high-quality replacement batteries at a lower cost.

Gruber Motors also offers a range of parts and accessories for Tesla owners, including custom wheels, interior upgrades, and performance enhancements. The company is known for its attention to detail and quality workmanship, and is a trusted resource for Tesla owners looking to customize and upgrade their vehicles.

Gruber Motors is a well-respected company in the Tesla community, known for its expertise, quality work, and commitment to customer satisfaction.

CHAPTER 7

Electric Car Safety

In this chapter, we'll address common safety concerns about electric cars, including their handling and braking capabilities, their crash safety ratings, and their emergency response procedures. We'll also provide guidance on how to handle the battery in the event of a crash or other emergency situation. By the end of this chapter, readers will have a better understanding of the safety features and procedures associated with electric cars.

Electric cars are becoming increasingly popular due to their environmental benefits and low operating costs. However, safety is always a top concern for drivers, and it's important to understand the safety features of electric cars before making a purchase.

One of the most notable electric car manufacturers is Tesla, which has made headlines for its safety ratings. The Tesla Model 3, for example, has received a 5-star safety rating from both the National Highway Traffic Safety Administration (NHTSA) and the European New Car Assessment Programme (Euro NCAP). The Model S and Model X have also received high safety ratings.

Tesla's vehicles are designed with safety in mind, incorporating features such as:

Battery placement: Tesla's battery is located beneath the car's floor, which helps to lower the center of gravity and reduce the risk of rollovers.

Crash avoidance features: Tesla's Autopilot system includes features such as adaptive cruise control and automatic emergency braking, which can help prevent accidents.

Structural design: Tesla's vehicles are designed with a strong frame and crumple zones, which can help absorb energy in the event of a collision.

Airbags: Tesla's vehicles are equipped with multiple airbags, including front, side, and curtain airbags.

While Tesla's safety ratings are impressive, it's worth noting that other electric cars have also received high safety ratings. The Audi e-tron, for example, has received a 5-star safety rating from the NHTSA, and the Chevrolet Bolt has received a 5-star rating from Euro NCAP.

It's important to research the safety ratings and features of any electric car before making a purchase. Some factors to consider include:

Crash test ratings: Check the safety ratings from organizations such as the NHTSA, Euro NCAP, and the Insurance Institute for Highway Safety (IIHS).

Safety features: Look for features such as adaptive cruise control, automatic emergency braking, and lane departure warning.

Battery placement: Consider the placement of the battery, as this can affect the car's center of gravity and rollover risk.

Structural design: Look for a car with a strong frame and crumple zones, which can help absorb energy in the event of a collision.

Tesla is always pushing the boundaries when it comes to automotive safety, and software and AI are key components of their strategy. Here are some ways Tesla is working to improve safety through these technologies:

Autopilot: Tesla's Autopilot system uses cameras, radar, and sensors to help drivers avoid accidents and stay safe on the road. The system can automatically steer, accelerate, and brake in certain situations, and it constantly monitors the surrounding environment to detect potential hazards.

Over-the-air updates: Tesla's software is constantly evolving, and the company can push updates to vehicles over the air, just like a smartphone. This means that safety features and improvements can be added to Tesla vehicles even after they have been purchased.

AI-powered collision avoidance: Tesla is working on advanced collision avoidance systems that use AI to predict potential accidents and take action to avoid them. For example, the system could automatically brake or steer to avoid a collision, even if the driver doesn't react in time.

Fleet learning: Tesla's fleet of vehicles is constantly collecting data and sending it back to the company for analysis. This data can be used to improve safety features and make the Autopilot system more effective at avoiding accidents.

Overall, Tesla's use of software and AI is helping to make their vehicles some of the safest on the road. As the technology continues to evolve, we can expect even more innovative safety features from this groundbreaking company.

> *In conclusion, electric cars are generally safe and offer many features to help prevent accidents. Tesla's safety ratings are impressive, but it's important to research and compare the safety features of any electric car before making a purchase.*

CHAPTER 8

Driving with the Power of the Sun

Driving a battery electric vehicle (BEV) with the power of the sun is an exciting concept that is gaining momentum as more people embrace renewable energy. With solar panels on your home or business, you can generate electricity to power your BEV, making transportation both sustainable and cost-effective.

To drive a BEV with solar power, you will need to install solar panels on your property. The panels will capture energy from the sun and convert it into electricity that can be used to power your home and charge your BEV. By using renewable energy to power your vehicle, you can reduce your carbon footprint and save money on fuel costs.

One of the benefits of driving a BEV with solar power is that you can potentially drive for free. If your solar panels generate enough energy to power both your home and your car, you may not have to pay for electricity at all. In some cases, you may even be able to sell excess energy back to the grid, generating additional income.

In addition to cost savings, driving a BEV with solar power can also help to reduce our dependence on fossil fuels. By using renewable energy to power our vehicles, we can reduce air pollution and combat climate change.

Looking to the future, the concept of free transportation is becoming increasingly popular. With the rise of shared mobility services such as ride-sharing and car-sharing, it's possible that transportation could one day be completely free. Companies such as Tesla and Uber are already exploring the concept of autonomous vehicles, which could reduce the cost of transportation even further.

In a future where transportation is free, the benefits would be far-reaching. Not only would it help to reduce the financial burden on individuals and families, but it could also help to reduce traffic congestion and improve air quality in urban areas. Additionally, free transportation could provide greater access to jobs, education, and healthcare for those who may not be able to afford it otherwise.

In conclusion, driving a BEV with solar power is an exciting concept that has the potential to transform the way we think about transportation. By harnessing the power of the sun, we can reduce our carbon footprint and potentially drive for free. Looking to the future, the concept of free transportation could have far-reaching benefits for society as a whole.

MY EXPERIENCE WITH SOLAR CHARGING

Picture this: I was cruising down the road in my trusty Tesla Model S (that little dark car on the following photo) on my way from Las Vegas to California when I pulled up to a Tesla Supercharger station near Baker, CA. As soon as I stepped out of the car, I was blown away by what I saw. The massive lot was filled with over 50 charging stalls and an absolutely enormous solar roof. It was like nothing I'd ever seen before!

After doing some digging, I found out that these solar-powered Supercharger stations are a crucial part of Tesla's plan to use renewable energy to power their electric cars. Depending on the size of the solar panels, location, and weather conditions, these stations can produce anywhere from 200-250 kW of power per day on average. That's enough energy to power several electric cars and is a major step forward in creating a more sustainable and eco-friendly transportation system.

On the day I visited, I was the only one charging my car, so it's highly likely that my car was 100% charged by the power of the sun. And to top it off, I have free supercharging on my Tesla account, so I didn't even have to pay a penny for my "refill"!

I truly believe that, with the proper economic models in place, we can create a future where renewable energy from the sun is not only the norm but also affordable and accessible to all. And with amazing innovations like Tesla's solar-powered Supercharger stations, that future is closer than ever.

Supercharger near Baker, CA

SOLAR POWERED EVS

There are several companies that develop cars that can be charged by the sun when parked and while driving.

Aptera

Aptera is an American electric vehicle (EV) company that specializes in the design and production of highly-efficient and environmentally-friendly EVs. The company was founded in 2006 and is based in San Diego, California.

Aptera's vehicles are designed to be as aerodynamic as possible, which helps to reduce drag and increase range. The company's first model, the Aptera 2 Series, featured a three-wheeled design and was capable of achieving up to 200 miles of range on a single charge. The vehicle was designed to be lightweight, with a composite body and a low-drag shape that helped to reduce energy consumption.

Aptera has continued to innovate in the EV space, and in 2020 the company unveiled a new model, the Aptera Sol. The Aptera Sol is a solar-electric vehicle, which means that it is equipped with a solar panel array that can help to recharge the battery and extend the vehicle's range. The company claims that the Aptera Sol is capable of achieving up to 1,000 miles of range on a single charge, thanks in part to its solar charging capabilities.

In addition to its focus on sustainability and efficiency, Aptera is also committed to safety. The company's vehicles are equipped with a range of safety features, including a high-strength safety cage, airbags, and a driver-assistance system that can help to prevent accidents.

Overall, Aptera is an innovative and forward-thinking company that is focused on producing efficient, sustainable, and safe electric vehicles. With its unique approach to design and its commitment to environmental responsibility, Aptera is poised to be a major player in the rapidly growing EV market.

Sono Motors

Sono Motors is a German-based electric vehicle (EV) company that was founded in 2016. The company is best known for its product, the Sion, which is a concept for a solar-electric vehicle designed for urban driving.

The Sion is based on a concept for a unique vehicle that is equipped with solar panels integrated into its exterior, which can help to recharge the battery and extend the vehicle's range. The car is also equipped with a range of other sustainability features, including a vegan interior and a moss-based air filtration system.

In addition to its focus on sustainability, the Sion is also designed for practicality and affordability. The car is designed for urban driving, with a compact size that makes it easy to navigate through traffic and park in tight spaces. The Sion is also designed to be affordable, with a base price that is significantly lower than many other EVs on the market.

Sono Motors has received significant interest from customers and investors, and has raised more than €50 million in funding to date. The company has also patented several solar cell technologies for transportation and secured several partnerships with automotive suppliers, which intended to help to bring the Sion to market.

However, in early 2023, Sono Motors abandoned the Sion project and is offering its patents and other assets to other car companies and investors. Sono Motors is now focused exclusively on solar cell development.

> *Overall, Sono Motors had a promising EV concept that was focused on sustainability, affordability, and practicality. With its unique solar-electric technology and commitment to environmental responsibility, the company was well-positioned to be a major player in the rapidly growing EV market.*

CHAPTER 9
Electric Cars and Your Wallet

What are the economic benefits of owning an electric car in more detail? We'll discuss the cost of ownership, including purchase price, maintenance, and fuel costs. We'll also provide an overview of government incentives and tax credits that can help offset the cost of owning an electric car. Additionally, we'll address some common misconceptions about the cost of electric cars and provide real-world examples of electric car ownership.

Overview

Category	Battery Electric Vehicle (BEV)	Gas Car
Purchase price	Since 2023, EVs start to become much cheaper than gas cars.	Generally higher than BEVs
Fuel cost	Much lower than gas cars, as electricity is cheaper than gasoline	Higher than BEVs, as gasoline is more expensive
Maintenance cost	Generally lower than gas cars, as EVs have fewer moving parts and require less maintenance	Generally higher than EVs, as gas cars have more moving parts and require more maintenance
Tax incentives	Eligible for federal and state tax credits and rebates, which can help offset the higher purchase price	No tax incentives for gas cars
Resale value	Generally higher than gas cars, as battery technology is evolving rapidly	Generally lower than EVs, as gas cars have many more parts that can break as they get older.

Purchasing Price

Hold onto your hats, folks - the electric vehicle (EV) revolution is about to get a whole lot cheaper! At the Tesla Investor Day on March 1st, 2023, the company announced that it's planning to slash the production cost of its new model line by a whopping 50%. That means that you could soon be driving away in a brand new Tesla for as little as $20,000 - say what?!

But that's not all - with competition from China heating up, EV prices could continue to drop even further. This is seriously bad news for gas-guzzling cars, which might be feeling a bit nervous right about now. Could we be witnessing the end of an era? Only time will tell, but one thing's for sure: the future of transportation is looking brighter (and more affordable) than ever before. Get ready to charge up and hit the road!

What about Charging Costs (Fuel Costs)

I have been cruising in my Tesla Model S for four months. The following three screenshots from my Tesla App show that I have saved over $1,200 since I purchased the car compared to driving a gasoline car. The right screenshot shows the daily Level 2 and supercharging activities. Based on these stats, I might be saving as much for transportation as I would pay monthly to finance the car. So, it's a free car.

My personal charging savings based on my Tesla App

For maintainance and tax incentives, please refer to the maintanance chapter.

Resale Value

When it comes to buying a new car, many people consider the resale value as an important factor. And when it comes to electric vehicles (EVs), there's good news: they tend to hold their value quite well.

One reason for this is that EV technology is still relatively new, and there is a growing demand for these vehicles as more people become interested in sustainable transportation. Additionally, EVs have lower maintenance costs than traditional gas-powered cars, which can make them more attractive to buyers in the used car market.

Another factor that can affect the resale value of an EV is the battery. As the battery degrades over time, the range and performance of the vehicle can be impacted, which can lower its value. However, many EV manufacturers offer battery warranties that can help to reassure buyers and maintain the value of the vehicle.

Of course, the resale value of an EV will ultimately depend on a number of factors, including the make and model, the condition of the vehicle, and the demand in the local market. However, as EVs become more mainstream and more people make the switch to electric, it's likely that their resale value will continue to hold steady or even increase over time. So if you're in the market for a new car and considering an EV, rest assured that it's a smart investment that will hold its value well.

In conclusion, EVs have the potential to make transportation effectively free in a few years.

CHAPTER 10

Overcoming Range Anxiety

In this chapter, we'll address one of the most common concerns about electric cars - range anxiety.

Range anxiety is a term used to describe the fear or concern that an electric vehicle (EV) driver experiences when they are worried about running out of battery power and being stranded without a charging station nearby. This anxiety can arise due to a number of factors, such as the limited range of some EVs, the scarcity of charging infrastructure in some areas, and the fear of not being able to find a charging station when needed.

For some drivers, range anxiety can be a significant barrier to the adoption of electric vehicles. This anxiety can be exacerbated by the fact that EVs typically take longer to charge than it takes to fill up a traditional gasoline-powered vehicle, and that some charging stations may not be working properly or may be occupied when needed.

However, as EV technology continues to improve and charging infrastructure becomes more widespread, range anxiety is becoming less of a concern for many drivers. With the development of longer-range batteries and faster charging options, many modern EVs are capable of driving hundreds of miles on a single charge, making them more practical for longer trips.

Additionally, the growth of charging infrastructure, including public charging stations and home charging options, has made it easier for EV drivers to find and use charging stations when needed. As a result, range anxiety is becoming less of a barrier to the widespread adoption of electric vehicles, and EVs are becoming an increasingly viable and sustainable transportation option for drivers around the world.

TECHNOLOGY

Tesla has developed several strategies to help alleviate range anxiety for its drivers. Some of these strategies include:

Supercharging network: Tesla has developed a proprietary network of Supercharger stations, which are strategically located along major travel routes and in densely populated areas. These stations can provide up to 170 miles of range in as little as 30 minutes of charging, and are often located near amenities such as restaurants and shopping centers, making them convenient for drivers on long trips.

Range estimation: Tesla vehicles are equipped with sophisticated range estimation software, which takes into account factors such as driving style, terrain, and weather conditions to provide drivers with an accurate estimate of their remaining range. This helps drivers to plan their trips and avoid running out of battery power.

Navigation system: Tesla's navigation system is designed to help drivers plan their trips, taking into account the location of charging stations and the vehicle's current battery charge level. The navigation system can also provide real-time information on the availability of charging stations and the estimated time required to charge the vehicle.

Over-the-air updates: Tesla can provide over-the-air software updates to its vehicles, which can improve the accuracy of the range estimation and provide additional features to help drivers manage their energy usage.

> *Overall, Tesla has developed a comprehensive suite of strategies to help alleviate range anxiety for its drivers. By providing a network of fast-charging stations, accurate range estimation software, and a sophisticated navigation system, Tesla is helping to make electric vehicles a more practical and convenient transportation option for drivers around the world.*

BATTERY / RANGE DISPLAY

Every electric vehicle has a battery charge display that shows the remaining charge in percentage or in miles/km.

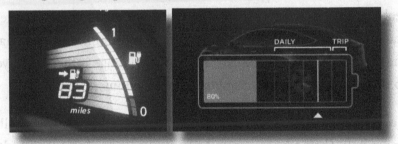

Battery Charge Display in a Nissan Leaf and a Tesla Model S

The EV software calculates contantly the remaining range based on several factors, including:

- **Battery capacity:** The total energy storage capacity of the battery pack in kilowatt-hours (kWh) is the primary factor in determining the range of an electric car. A higher capacity battery pack can store more energy, allowing for a longer driving range.

- **Driving style and conditions:** The way the driver accelerates, brakes, and drives affects the energy consumption of the car. Driving at high speeds, frequent acceleration, and hard braking consume more energy and decrease the range of the car. Similarly, driving in extreme temperatures, such as extreme cold or heat, can also affect the range of the car.
- **Vehicle weight:** The weight of the vehicle affects its energy consumption. Heavier vehicles require more energy to move, reducing their range.
- **Terrain:** Driving on hilly or mountainous terrain requires more energy to maintain speed, reducing the range of the car.
- **Accessories and features:** Using accessories like air conditioning, heating, and entertainment systems can increase energy consumption and reduce the range of the car.

Every electric car uses more or less sophisticated onboard systems to calculate their range based on these factors. The systems use real-time data from various sensors and inputs, including battery state-of-charge, driving speed, and energy consumption, to estimate the remaining range of the car. The estimated range is then displayed to the driver on the car's dashboard or infotainment system.

Both displaying the percentage of the battery and the range in miles or km have their advantages and disadvantages, and the choice ultimately comes down to personal preference.

Displaying the percentage of the battery provides a clear and accurate representation of the current state-of-charge of the battery. It allows drivers to know exactly how much energy is remaining in the battery and when it needs to be recharged. This information is particularly useful for drivers who are familiar with their car's energy consumption and range, as they can estimate how far they can travel based on the remaining battery percentage.

On the other hand, displaying the range in miles or km provides a more tangible and relatable metric for drivers. It shows drivers how far they can travel on the remaining battery charge and helps them plan their trips accordingly. This information is particularly useful for drivers who are less familiar with their car's energy consumption and range, as it provides a more intuitive understanding of the car's capabilities.

Ultimately, the decision between displaying the percentage of the battery or the range in miles comes down to personal preference and driving habits. Some drivers may prefer the precision and accuracy of the battery percentage, while others may prefer the more intuitive and relatable metric of the range in miles.

THE TESLA CONSUMPTION GRAPH

To reduce range anxiety, some EVs provide a consumption graph. The Tesla consumption graph, which is displayed in every Tesla vehicle, is a tool that allows drivers to visualize their vehicle's energy usage and range in real time. The graph is divided into three sections, with the top section showing the energy consumption of the vehicle, the middle section showing the estimated range, and the bottom section showing the energy regeneration from braking.

In the top section of the graph, the driver can see how much energy the vehicle is consuming in real time, measured in kilowatts (kW). The graph shows a line that represents the average energy consumption over the past 5, 15, or 30 miles (depending on the user's settings), as well as a bar that shows the instantaneous energy consumption. The graph also includes a target line, which represents the energy usage required to reach the driver's desired destination based on the current battery charge level.

The middle section of the graph shows the estimated range of the vehicle, based on the current energy consumption and the remaining battery charge. The range estimate is shown in miles or kilometers, depending on the user's settings.

The bottom section of the graph shows the energy regeneration from braking, measured in kilowatts. When the driver applies the brakes, the vehicle's kinetic energy is converted into electrical energy and stored in the battery. The graph shows the amount of energy being regenerated in real time, and the driver can use this information to optimize their driving style and maximize the energy regeneration.

Overall, the Tesla consumption graph is a powerful tool for helping drivers to understand and manage their vehicle's energy usage and range. By using this information to adjust their driving habits and optimize their energy usage, Tesla drivers can reduce their environmental impact and save money on fuel costs.

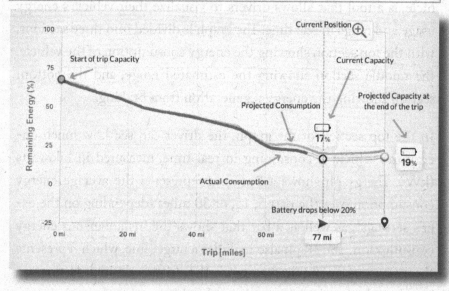

CHAPTER 11

Driving an Electric Car

Elon Musk, CEO of Tesla: "Driving a gasoline sports car is going to feel like a steam engine with a side of quiche."

Arnold Schwarzenegger, former Governor of California: "Driving an electric car is a blast - with instant torque and a quiet ride, it's a great experience."

Prince Albert II of Monaco: "Electric cars are the future of the automobile. They have the ability to power the world with clean energy, and they can be a lot of fun to drive."

Robert Llewellyn, host of "Fully Charged" YouTube channel: "The driving experience of an electric car is like nothing else. Instant torque, quiet running, and smooth power delivery make it a joy to drive."

Lewis Hamilton, Formula One driver: "Driving an electric car is such a unique and exciting experience. It's fast, it's quiet, and it's really the future."

Barack Obama, former President of the United States: "Electric cars are not a passing fad - they're a key part of our clean energy future. And they're fun to drive, too."

Richard Branson, entrepreneur and founder of Virgin Group: "Driving an electric car is a game-changer. The instant acceleration and smooth ride are amazing, and the fact that it's so much better for the environment is a huge bonus."

DRIVING TIPS AND BEST PRACTICES

Driving an electric vehicle (EV) can be a little different from driving a traditional gasoline-powered car. Here are some driving tips to help you get the most out of your EV:

Use regenerative braking: Many EVs have regenerative braking, which means the car recovers some of the energy lost during braking and uses it to recharge the battery. This can help extend your range and reduce wear on your brake pads. Practice using regenerative braking by gently lifting your foot off the accelerator pedal when you need to slow down.

Plan your routes: One of the most important considerations when driving an EV is range. Make sure to plan your routes carefully and use apps or websites that can help you find charging stations along the way. Try to avoid routes with steep inclines or frequent stop-and-go traffic, as these conditions can use up more energy.

Because route planning with a Tesla is a unique feature, I decided to add this short description of the system. Thanks to its built-in navigation system that can automatically plan your route and factor in necessary charging stops along the way. When planning a trip, you can simply input your destination into the navigation system and it will calculate the most efficient route, taking into account the range of your Tesla and the location of available charging stations.

The navigation system will also show you the available charging options along your route, including Tesla's extensive Supercharger network, allowing you to make the most informed decision about where to stop for a charge. The Supercharger network is the largest and most reliable charging network in the world, and it continues to expand rapidly, providing Tesla drivers with the ability to travel long distances with ease.

> *Additionally, Tesla's navigation system is continually updated with real-time traffic data, allowing it to provide you with the most accurate and up-to-date route information. And if you need to change your plans mid-trip, the system can quickly recalculate your route and charging stops to get you back on track.*
>
> *With Tesla's comprehensive navigation system, planning a route and finding charging stations along the way is a seamless and stress-free experience, ensuring that you can enjoy your trip and arrive at your destination with ease.*

Be gentle with the accelerator: Rapid acceleration can use up more energy and reduce your range. Try to accelerate gradually and avoid sudden bursts of speed. This will help you conserve energy and extend your range.

Keep an eye on your battery level: Most EVs have a dashboard display that shows your battery level and estimated range. Make sure to keep an eye on this display and plan your charging stops accordingly. If you're running low on battery, find a charging station as soon as possible.

Pre-condition your car: Many EVs have a pre-conditioning feature that allows you to heat or cool the car before you start driving. This can help reduce the amount of energy needed to maintain a comfortable temperature inside the car.

Drive in eco mode: Many EVs have an eco mode that can help you conserve energy. This mode limits acceleration and adjusts other settings to maximize efficiency.

Take advantage of public charging stations: Public charging stations can be a great resource for EV drivers. Make sure to plan your routes to include stops at charging stations, and take advantage of the time to grab a coffee or check your email.

By following these tips, you can help ensure that your EV driving experience is as efficient and enjoyable as possible.

USING REGENERATIVE BRAKING

Regenerative braking is a key feature of electric vehicles (EVs), and it can help drivers save energy and extend their driving range. Here's how it works:

When you apply the brakes in a traditional gasoline-powered car, the kinetic energy of the car is converted into heat produced by the brake pads and dissipated into the environment. With regenerative braking, however, the electric motor in an EV can act as a generator, using the car's kinetic energy to recharge the battery instead of wasting it as heat.

Below is a photo of my car screen while going down a longer hill in the California mountains. For a distance of about five miles, I was able to charge the battery from 17% full to 19% full. You can see the amount of charging on the right part of the graph that goes below the zero Wh/mi axis. A negative consumption indicates that energy flows from the motor to the battery.

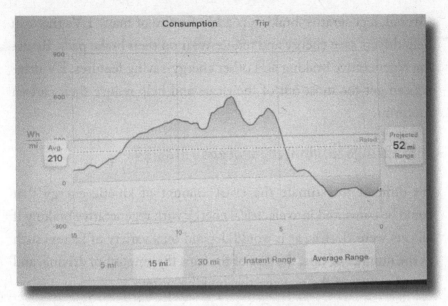

This process is most effective when you use the brake pedal lightly, as the regenerative braking system won't be able to capture all the energy if you brake too hard. To maximize the benefits of regenerative braking, try to anticipate stops and slow down gradually instead of braking suddenly.

Some EVs also have a feature called "*one-pedal driving*," which can be enabled in the settings. This feature allows you to drive using only the accelerator pedal, and the car will automatically slow down when you lift your foot off the pedal, using regenerative braking to slow the car down and recover energy. This can help you reduce wear on your brake pads and save energy.

In addition to regenerative braking, some EVs also have an "eco" mode that can help you conserve energy. This mode adjusts the car's acceleration and other settings to maximize efficiency and reduce energy consumption. Using eco mode in combination with regenerative braking can help you get the most out of your EV and extend your driving range.

Overall, regenerative braking is a key feature of many EVs that can help drivers save energy and reduce wear on their brake pads. By using regenerative braking and other energy-saving features, EV drivers can get the most out of their cars and help reduce their carbon footprint.

Fuel Savings through regenerative braking

It's difficult to estimate the exact amount of kinetic energy that could be converted into electrical energy with regenerative braking if all cars were electric, as it would depend on a variety of factors such as the number of cars, the size of the cars, the amount of driving, and the efficiency of the regenerative braking system.

However, some estimates suggest that if all cars in the United States were electric and equipped with regenerative braking, the energy recovered through regenerative braking could be as much as 15% of the total energy used for transportation. In 2021, distillate fuel consumption by the U.S. transportation sector, which is essentially diesel and gas fuel, was about 46.82 billion gallons (1.11 billion barrels), an average of about 128 million gallons per day. 15% less fuel would equate to *19.2 million gallons less fuel per day*! This will have a significant impact on reducing greenhouse gas emissions and combating climate change. (Source: https://www.eia.gov/energyexplained/diesel-fuel/use-of-diesel.php)

It's worth noting that regenerative braking is just one of the many benefits of electric vehicles, which also include reduced emissions, lower operating costs, and improved performance. As more people switch to electric vehicles, the potential for regenerative braking and other energy-saving features to make a difference in the environment will only continue to grow.

SELF-DRIVING CARS AND TESLA'S FSD BETA

Self-driving vehicles, or autonomous vehicles, are the future of transportation. They have the potential to revolutionize the way we travel, making it safer, more efficient, and more convenient. Tesla is one of the leading companies in the development of self-driving technology. The company's Full Self-Driving (FSD) beta is a major step forward in this direction.

The FSD beta is an advanced system that uses artificial intelligence and machine learning to enable Teslas to drive themselves without human intervention. The FSD beta utilizes a network of sensors, cameras, and radar to analyze the environment around the vehicle and make real-time decisions about how to navigate through it. This technology is still in the development stage and is not yet available to the general public.

The FSD beta development program is a way for Tesla to gather data and refine its self-driving technology. The program is available to a select group of Tesla owners who have signed up to participate. Participants are required to provide feedback on their experiences with the FSD beta, including any issues or bugs they encounter.

In addition to the FSD beta, Tesla's app is also a key part of the company's self-driving strategy. The app allows owners to remotely monitor and control their vehicles, including starting and stopping the car, opening and closing doors, and adjusting climate control settings. The app also provides real-time updates on the vehicle's location, battery charge level, and other important information.

Looking to the future, Tesla plans to use the app to enable robotaxis, or self-driving taxis. The idea is that Tesla owners will be able to earn money by allowing their vehicles to operate as robotaxis when

The Future is Electric

they are not in use. The app would allow users to easily request a ride and pay for the service, while Tesla would handle the logistics of dispatching the vehicle and managing the fleet.

Overall, self-driving technology and Tesla's FSD beta are exciting developments that could have a major impact on the future of transportation. While there are still many challenges to overcome before fully autonomous vehicles become a reality, the progress made so far is impressive, and the potential benefits are significant.

CHAPTER 12

The EV Lifestyle

The EV (electric vehicle) lifestyle is centered around driving and owning an electric car, and it encompasses a range of practices and behaviors that reflect a commitment to sustainability and environmental responsibility. Here are some key features of the EV lifestyle:

Emphasis on sustainability: One of the main reasons people choose to drive electric cars is to reduce their carbon footprint and promote sustainability. EV drivers are often passionate about the environment and make efforts to reduce their energy consumption and carbon emissions in other aspects of their lives as well.

Awareness of energy usage: EV drivers are often very conscious of their energy usage and make an effort to reduce their energy consumption. This might include monitoring their home energy usage, using energy-efficient appliances, and taking steps to conserve energy wherever possible.

Use of renewable energy: Many EV drivers choose to power their cars using renewable energy sources such as solar or wind power. This helps to further reduce their carbon footprint and promote sustainable living.

Community building: The EV lifestyle often involves a strong sense of community and connection with other EV drivers. This might involve attending EV events or meetups, sharing information and tips with other drivers, and advocating for policies that promote sustainable transportation.

Emphasis on technology: EV drivers are often interested in the latest technologies and innovations in the electric car industry. This might include following the latest news about EVs, exploring new features and apps related to EVs, and participating in discussions and forums about the future of electric transportation.

Focus on efficiency: EV drivers often focus on efficiency in all aspects of their lives, from the way they drive to the way they charge their cars. This might include driving in eco mode, using regenerative braking, and optimizing charging schedules to reduce energy usage.

The EV lifestyle is centered around a commitment to sustainability, environmental responsibility, and the latest technology. It involves a sense of community and connection with other EV drivers, as well as a focus on energy efficiency and the use of renewable energy sources. As more people embrace the EV lifestyle, it has the potential to make a significant impact on reducing carbon emissions and promoting a more sustainable future.

PART THREE

THE FUTURE

CHAPTER 13

The Future of Electric Cars

In this chapter, we'll explore the future of electric cars, including advancements in technology and their potential impact on the transportation industry. We'll discuss the growing popularity of electric cars and the increasing availability of charging infrastructure, as well as the potential for self-driving electric cars. Additionally, we'll address some common concerns about the future of electric cars, such as their impact on the power grid, and provide insights into how these issues are being addressed.

TRENDS AND PROJECTIONS

The trends and projections for electric vehicles (EVs) are generally positive, with significant growth expected in the coming years. Here are some of the key trends and projections for EVs:

Increased adoption: EV sales have been growing steadily in recent years, and many analysts predict that this trend will continue. In 2020, global EV sales increased by 43% compared to the previous year, and some projections suggest that EVs could account for up to 50% of all new car sales by 2030.

New models: Many automakers are investing in EV technology and introducing new models to their lineups. This is expected to help drive adoption of EVs by offering consumers more choices and improving the overall appeal of electric transportation.

Battery technology: Battery technology is a key driver of EV adoption, and many companies are investing in research and development to improve battery performance, reduce costs, and increase durability. This is expected to result in longer-range EVs with lower costs, making them more accessible to a wider range of consumers.

Charging infrastructure: The availability of charging infrastructure is another key factor in the adoption of EVs. Governments and private companies are investing in new charging infrastructure to support the growing number of EVs on the road. Some projections suggest that there could be over 50 million public charging points worldwide by 2030.

Government incentives: Many governments offer incentives to encourage the adoption of EVs, such as tax credits, rebates, and grants. These incentives are expected to continue, and some analysts predict that they could be expanded to include additional benefits such as free parking and toll exemptions.

Overall, the trends and projections for EVs are positive, with strong growth expected in the coming years. As battery technology improves, charging infrastructure expands, and government incentives continue, EVs are likely to become an increasingly common sight on roads around the world.

VIRTUAL POWER PLANS (VPP) AND EVS

A VPP, or Virtual Power Plant, is a network of decentralized power sources that can be coordinated to function as a single, large-scale power plant. This includes distributed energy resources like rooftop solar panels, battery storage systems, and electric vehicles (EVs) with bidirectional charging capabilities.

By incorporating EVs into VPPs, the electric grid can benefit from increased flexibility, resilience, and efficiency. EVs can serve as both consumers and suppliers of energy, depending on their state of charge and the needs of the grid. When plugged in, EVs can draw power from the grid to charge their batteries, but they can also supply power back to the grid during times of high demand or to support grid stability during emergencies.

The bidirectional charging capability of EVs allows them to become a valuable resource for managing peak demand and balancing the variability of renewable energy sources like solar and wind. During periods of low demand, EVs can charge their batteries with excess energy from the grid or from on-site renewable sources. During periods of high demand, such as hot summer afternoons when air conditioning use is high, EVs can supply power back to the grid to help meet the demand.

In addition, the use of VPPs can help to reduce the need for costly new transmission and distribution infrastructure, as well as reduce the need for new power plants. This can result in lower electricity costs for consumers and fewer greenhouse gas emissions from the electric grid.

The incorporation of EVs into VPPs is a promising approach to improving the reliability, efficiency, and sustainability of the electric grid.

THE S-CURVE FOR EV ADOPTION

An adoption S-curve is a graphical representation of the rate of adoption of a new technology or innovation over time. The S-curve typically shows an initial slow rate of adoption, followed by a period of rapid growth, and then a plateau as the technology reaches saturation.

The adoption S-curve is often used by analysts and researchers to model the adoption of new technologies, including electric vehicles, and to make predictions about future growth and adoption rates. By analyzing historical adoption data and fitting mathematical models to that data, analysts can estimate the timing and rate of future adoption, which can be useful for planning and investment decisions.

The S-curve is named for its shape, which resembles the letter S. The initial slow growth phase is characterized by a relatively small number of early adopters, who are typically enthusiasts and innovators. The rapid growth phase is characterized by a larger number of early adopters, as well as a growing number of mainstream consumers who are starting to become interested in the technology. The saturation phase is characterized by a leveling off of the adoption rate, as most potential adopters have already adopted the technology.

The adoption S-curve can be influenced by a variety of factors, including technological advancements, government policies, public perception, and infrastructure development. As these factors change over time, the rate of adoption can accelerate or slow down, leading to changes in the shape and timing of the S-curve.

> *The adoption S-curve is a useful tool for understanding and predicting the rate of adoption of new technologies, including electric vehicles, and can help guide decision-making and investment strategies.*

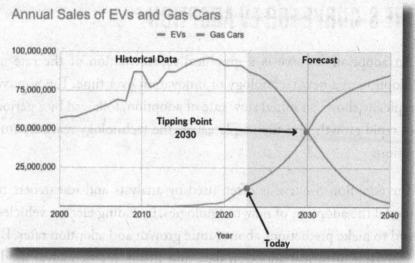

Annual production and sales of EVs and gas cars from 2000 to 2022 as publicly available. Grey area: production rates from 2022 to 2040 are Author's forecast based on a collection of expert's opinions including Bloomberg News.

We have experienced a very similar development when cars took over the streets and replacing horses in the very early 1900s.

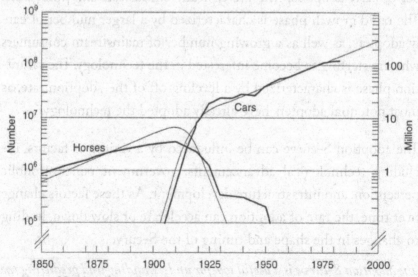

Number of non-farm draft horses and automobiles in the USA.
Source: Nakićenović, 1997 (core.ac.uk/download/pdf/44737907.pdf)

INNOVATIONS AND NEW TECHNOLOGIES

In the next 20 years, we can expect to see a range of new innovations and technologies in the field of electric vehicle development. Here are some of the most promising developments and trends to watch for:

- **Improved battery technology:** Battery technology is a key area of focus for EV developers, and we can expect to see continued improvements in battery performance, range, and charging times. New battery chemistries, such as solid-state batteries, may also become more viable, offering even greater improvements in energy density and safety.

- **Vehicle-to-grid (V2G) technology:** V2G technology allows electric vehicles to store and discharge electricity back to the grid, making them an important part of a flexible and sustainable energy system. This technology could become more widespread in the coming years, with more EV owners using their vehicles as part of a decentralized energy grid.

- **Autonomous driving:** Autonomous driving technology is advancing rapidly, and it is likely that more EVs will be equipped with self-driving capabilities in the future. This could lead to increased safety, reduced traffic congestion, and greater energy efficiency.

- **Improved charging infrastructure:** As the number of EVs on the road continues to grow, we can expect to see increased investment in charging infrastructure. This could include faster and more convenient charging options, such as wireless charging and high-speed charging stations.

Looking for a new car used to be all about the features, quality, and price tag. But when it comes to electric vehicles, there's a new kid on the block: the charging network. It might not be as flashy as a sports car or as luxurious as a high-end sedan, but when you're on the road with an electric vehicle, it's the charging network that truly matters.

Think about it: what good is a fancy car if you can't charge it properly when you need to? That's why Tesla has been leading the way in building the most reliable and widely available charging infrastructure around the world. They've realized that the key to making electric vehicles a practical and convenient option is to have a robust and user-friendly charging network that can get you where you need to go, without any hassle.

- **Lack of investment:** One of the biggest barriers to improving EV charging infrastructure is the lack of investment in this area. Installing and maintaining charging stations can be expensive, and many businesses and governments have been hesitant to make large investments in this technology, especially if they don't see an immediate return on investment.

- **Regulatory barriers:** There are also regulatory barriers that can slow down the deployment of EV charging infrastructure. For example, some cities or regions may require permits or approvals for charging stations, which can be time-consuming and expensive to obtain.

- **Car manufacturers' priorities:** Some car manufacturers may be slowing down the process of improving EV charging infrastructure because they see it as a lower priority than other aspects of EV development, such as improving battery technology or increasing production volume.

- **Different charging standards:** Finally, another challenge to developing EV charging infrastructure is the existence of different charging standards. Tesla uses superior and very reliable charging connectors, while others use open standards like CCS or CHAdeMO. This can make it more difficult to install and maintain charging stations that are compatible with all EVs.

Overall, improving EV charging infrastructure requires a combination of investment, supportive regulations, and collaboration between car manufacturers and other stakeholders. While progress has been slow in some areas, there are signs of improvement, and many experts predict that the adoption of EVs will continue to accelerate in the coming years.

- **Innovative designs and materials:** EV manufacturers are exploring new materials and design strategies to make vehicles lighter, more efficient, and more sustainable. This could lead to new vehicle designs and form factors that are optimized for electric propulsion, as well as new materials that are more environmentally friendly and easier to recycle.
- **Vehicle-to-everything (V2X) connectivity:** V2X technology allows EVs to communicate with other vehicles, pedestrians, and infrastructure, enabling a range of new applications and services. This could include improved traffic flow, advanced safety features, and new mobility services that are tailored to individual needs.

We can expect to see a range of exciting developments and innovations in the field of EV development in the next 20 years. These innovations could help to make EVs more convenient, more efficient, and more sustainable, making them an increasingly attractive option for consumers and businesses alike.

IMPACT ON THE ENVIRONMENT AND SOCIETY

The impact of the new developments and innovations in the field of electric vehicle (EV) development is likely to be significant, both for the environment and for society as a whole. Here are some of the potential impacts that we can expect:

Reduced greenhouse gas emissions: As EVs become more efficient and as the electricity grid becomes increasingly powered by renewable energy, we can expect to see a significant reduction in greenhouse gas emissions from the transportation sector. This could help to mitigate the impacts of climate change and reduce air pollution in urban areas.

Improved air quality: With fewer tailpipe emissions, we can expect to see improvements in air quality, especially in cities and other urban areas. This could have significant health benefits, reducing the incidence of respiratory illnesses and other health problems associated with air pollution.

Changes in the energy industry: The widespread adoption of EVs is likely to have significant impacts on the energy industry, as the demand for electricity for transportation increases. This could lead to changes in the way electricity is generated and distributed, as well as new business models and revenue streams.

Changes in mobility patterns: As EVs become more common and as mobility services become more flexible and accessible, we can expect to see changes in the way people travel and use transportation. This could include more shared mobility options, as well as new forms of mobility that are tailored to individual needs and preferences.

Economic impacts: The transition to EVs is likely to have significant economic impacts, both positive and negative. On the one hand, there may be job losses in the traditional automotive industry, as well as in the fossil fuel sector. On the other hand, there may be new job opportunities in the EV manufacturing and maintenance sectors, as well as in the renewable energy industry.

> *Overall, the impact of the new developments and innovations in the field of EV development is likely to be far-reaching and significant, affecting everything from the environment and public health to the energy industry and the economy. As these changes unfold, it will be important to monitor and manage their impacts in order to ensure a sustainable and equitable transition to a more electric and sustainable transportation system.*

CHALLENGES AND OPPORTUNITIES

While the widespread adoption of electric vehicles (EVs) has the potential to bring many positive environmental and social benefits, there may also be negative impacts associated with the transition. Here are some potential negative impacts to consider:

Raw materials sourcing: EV batteries rely on a range of minerals and metals, such as lithium, cobalt, and nickel. The mining and extraction of these materials can have negative environmental impacts, including deforestation, habitat destruction, and water pollution. There are also concerns about human rights abuses and exploitation in the mining of these materials.

Battery disposal: At the end of their life cycle, EV batteries will need to be disposed of or recycled. If not managed properly, the disposal of large numbers of batteries could create significant waste management challenges and environmental hazards.

Energy demand: As the number of EVs on the road increases, so too will the demand for electricity. This could place strain on the electricity grid, especially if charging is concentrated at certain times of the day. It could also increase the demand for fossil fuels if the electricity is generated from non-renewable sources.

Equity and access: The switch to electric vehicles (EVs) may not benefit everyone equally due to disparities in access to sustainable transportation options and uneven distribution of charging infrastructure. While EVs have historically been more expensive than conventional cars, prices will go down to around $20,000 in the next few years, as predicted by ARK Investment Management based on Wright's Law, could make them affordable to about 80% of the population. Since 2012, EVs have gained market share at an expected rate considering their price point and the price elasticity of demand for vehicles.

Job losses: The transition to EVs is likely to have significant impacts on the automotive industry and other related sectors. This could lead to job losses and economic dislocation in some regions and industries, especially in areas where there is a high dependence on traditional automotive manufacturing.

Overall, while the transition to electric vehicles is likely to bring many positive benefits, it is important to consider and manage the potential negative impacts. By addressing these challenges, it may be possible to minimize the negative impacts and maximize the positive ones.

CHAPTER 14

Electric Cars and the Environment

In this chapter, we'll provide a more detailed exploration of the environmental benefits of electric cars. We'll discuss the impact of transportation on climate change and the importance of reducing greenhouse gas emissions. We'll also provide an overview of the manufacturing and disposal of electric car batteries, and discuss the role of renewable energy sources in powering electric cars. By the end of this chapter, readers will have a comprehensive understanding of the environmental impact of electric cars.

Electric vehicles (EVs) have the potential to significantly reduce the environmental impact of transportation, which is one of the largest contributors to global greenhouse gas (GHG) emissions. According to the International Energy Agency, the transportation sector accounts for nearly one-quarter of global GHG emissions, with road transportation being the largest contributor. As a result, reducing transportation emissions is a critical component of efforts to mitigate the impacts of climate change.

One of the primary environmental benefits of EVs is that they produce zero tailpipe emissions. This means that they do not release harmful pollutants, such as particulate matter, nitrogen oxides, and sulfur dioxide, which can contribute to air pollution and respiratory illnesses. In addition, because EVs can be charged using electricity from renewable sources, such as wind or solar power, they can help to reduce the carbon footprint of transportation.

The manufacturing and disposal of EV batteries can also have environmental impacts, but these impacts are generally smaller than those associated with traditional internal combustion engine (ICE) vehicles. EV batteries contain a range of materials, including lithium, cobalt, and nickel, which must be mined and extracted. However, these materials are used in relatively small quantities, and are becoming easier to recycle as recycling technology improves. In addition, as the market for EVs grows, it is likely that more sustainable and environmentally-friendly practices will be developed for sourcing and recycling battery materials.

The role of renewable energy sources in powering EVs is also an important consideration. In order for EVs to have the greatest environmental benefit, they must be powered by electricity generated from renewable sources. In recent years, the cost of renewable energy has decreased significantly, and as a result, renewable energy is becoming more competitive with traditional fossil fuels. As the share of renewable energy in the electricity grid grows, the environmental benefits of EVs will continue to increase.

Overall, the environmental benefits of electric cars are significant, and the adoption of EVs is an important component of efforts to reduce greenhouse gas emissions and mitigate the impacts of climate change. While there are still challenges to be addressed, such as the sustainable sourcing and disposal of battery materials, the potential benefits of EVs make them a promising technology for a more sustainable future.

CHAPTER 15

Conclusion and Resources

In conclusion, the future of electric vehicles is promising, and the impact of EVs on the environment, society, and the economy is significant. EVs have the potential to revolutionize transportation by reducing carbon emissions and improving air quality, while also decreasing our reliance on non-renewable sources of energy. The development of new technologies, such as longer-range batteries and faster charging systems, is making electric vehicles more practical and accessible to a wider range of consumers. Additionally, the deployment of smart grid technology and vehicle-to-grid systems has the potential to improve the stability and efficiency of the electric grid, while also reducing the cost of electricity for consumers.

However, there are still challenges to overcome, such as the availability of public charging infrastructure, the high initial cost of EVs, and the manufacturing and disposal of batteries. Governments, businesses, and individuals all have a role to play in promoting and supporting the adoption of EVs and advancing the development of sustainable transportation.

Overall, the continued growth and development of electric vehicles hold tremendous promise for a cleaner, more efficient, and more sustainable future. As we continue to innovate and evolve in this field, we have the opportunity to create a world that is not only better for ourselves, but also for generations to come.

ADDITIONAL RESOURCES FOR FURTHER LEARNING

There are many resources available for further learning about electric vehicles. Here are a few suggestions:

- The Electric Auto Association (EAA) is a non-profit organization dedicated to promoting electric vehicles. They provide information, resources, and events to help people learn more about EVs.
- Plug In America is another non-profit organization that provides resources and advocacy for EVs. They have a variety of educational materials, including videos, webinars, and guides.
- The U.S. Department of Energy has an extensive collection of resources on EVs, including information on charging, incentives, and technologies.
- The EV-focused media outlets, such as Electrek, InsideEVs, and CleanTechnica, provide news, reviews, and analysis on the latest developments in the EV industry.
- EV enthusiast groups on social media platforms like Facebook and Reddit can be a great way to connect with other EV owners and enthusiasts and learn from their experiences.
- Online courses, such as those offered by Udemy, Coursera, and edX, can provide in-depth education on specific topics related to EVs, such as battery technology or charging infrastructure.

Finally, attending auto shows and EV-focused events can provide hands-on experience with different EV models and technologies, as well as an opportunity to network with industry experts and other enthusiasts.

CALL TO ACTION FOR EMBRACING ELECTRIC CARS

Are you ready to take the leap and embrace the future of sustainable transportation? Electric cars are not only stylish and fun to drive, but they also provide countless benefits for our environment, health, and economy. By choosing an electric car, you are taking a step towards reducing your carbon footprint, improving air quality, and supporting the renewable energy industry, and on top of that, saving money.

But we can't do it alone. We need everyone's help to make this transition to electric cars a reality. Whether you are a driver, policymaker, or industry leader, we all have a role to play in building a cleaner and more sustainable future.

So, let's start by spreading the word about the benefits of electric cars and encouraging others to make the switch. Let's support and advocate for the expansion of public charging infrastructure and the implementation of policies that incentivize the adoption of electric cars. Let's demand that automakers invest in the development of new and better electric car models.

Together, we can create a world that is powered by clean and renewable energy. Are you ready to join the revolution?

PART THREE

APPENDIX

Used EV Car Guide

Buying a used electric vehicle (EV) can be a good option for several reasons. Here are a few:

Lower price: Used EVs are often significantly less expensive than new ones. This can make them an attractive option for buyers who are looking to save money or who want to try out an EV without investing a lot of money upfront.

Good battery life: One of the biggest concerns with EVs is the lifespan of the battery. However, many EV batteries have proven to be very durable and long-lasting. This means that used EVs can often still have plenty of life left in the battery, making them a smart investment.

Reduced depreciation: Like all cars, EVs lose value over time. However, the rate of depreciation for EVs tends to be slower than for gasoline-powered cars. This means that a used EV can retain more of its value than a used gas car, making it a better investment in the long run.

Environmental benefits: Buying a used EV can also have environmental benefits, as it helps to reduce the carbon footprint associated with new car production. By buying a used EV, you're making use of an existing resource and preventing the need for additional manufacturing.

Maintenance cost savings: EVs have fewer moving parts than gasoline-powered cars, which means they require less maintenance.

Buying a used EV can be a good option for those who want to save money, reduce their carbon footprint, and enjoy the benefits of electric transportation. With a range of affordable and reliable used EVs on the market, there's never been a better time to make the switch to electric. To find a used EV car guide, you can refer to various online resources that specialize in providing information and reviews on electric vehicles. Some popular websites and platforms include:

- **Kelley Blue Book (KBB)** - kbb.com offers comprehensive information on used electric vehicles, including their retail values, expert reviews, and buyer's guides.
- **Edmunds** - edmunds.com is another valuable resource for finding used EV car guides, providing reviews, comparisons, pricing information, and buying advice.
- **InsideEVs** - insideevs.com is dedicated to electric vehicles and offers news, reviews, and buying guides for used EVs.
- **Green Car Reports** - greencarreports.com. Green Car Reports focuses on green and eco-friendly vehicles, including electric vehicles. The site provides reviews, news, and used car buying guides for EVs.
- **Consumer Reports** - consumerreports.org is a well-known source for unbiased product reviews and ratings, including used electric vehicles. They offer comprehensive guides and advice for purchasing used EVs.
- **CarGurus** - cargurus.com is a car shopping website that provides listings for used EVs, including reviews, price comparisons, and a platform for connecting with sellers.

When searching for a used EV car guide, it's essential to consider multiple sources, read reviews, and compare the information provided to make an informed decision.

FAQs

Here are some frequently asked questions and their answers about electric cars:

How do I charge my electric car?

You can charge your electric car at home using a Level 1 or Level 2 charger, or at public charging stations using Level 2 or DC fast chargers. You can also use Tesla's supercharger network if you own a Tesla vehicle.

What is the range of an electric car?

The range of an electric car depends on the battery capacity, the driving style, and the weather conditions. Most electric cars have a range of between 100 and 300 miles on a single charge.

How long does it take to charge an electric car?

The charging time depends on the type of charger and the battery size. Level 1 chargers can take up to 12 hours to fully charge an EV, while Level 2 chargers can take 4-8 hours. DC fast chargers can charge an EV up to 80% in 30 minutes.

How much does it cost to charge an electric car?

The cost of charging an electric car varies depending on the electricity rates in your area and the size of your car's battery. On average, it costs about $0.12 per kilowatt-hour to charge an EV.

Do electric cars require regular maintenance?

Electric cars require less maintenance than gasoline cars because they have fewer moving parts. However, you still need to have your tires, brakes, and suspension system checked regularly, and the battery and cooling system need to be inspected periodically.

Can I drive an electric car in the rain or snow?

Yes, electric cars can be driven in the rain or snow, but you should take extra precautions because wet and icy roads can reduce your car's range and traction. EV manufacturers typically make sure the car batteries and electrical systems are properly insulated and sealed to prevent damage from moisture.

What happens if my electric car runs out of power?

If your electric car runs out of power, you will need to tow it to a charging station or a safe location where you can plug it in. You should always keep an eye on your car's battery level and plan your trips accordingly to avoid running out of power.

Are electric cars more expensive than gasoline cars?

Electric cars used to be generally more expensive than gasoline cars, but this is changing in 2023 because, fundamentally, EVs have less than half parts than gas cars and are easier to assemble. That's why they can be more cost-effective in the long run because they require less maintenance and have lower operating costs.

The price for new EVs has been steadily declining in recent years, and many experts predict that EVs will become cost-competitive with gas cars this year as some estimates suggest.

What is the lifespan of an electric car battery?

The lifespan of an electric car battery depends on the battery chemistry and the usage patterns. Most electric car batteries are designed to last for 8-10 years or 100,000-200,000 miles, but some can last longer with proper maintenance and care.

How eco-friendly are electric cars?

Unlike gasoline cars, EVs produce zero emissions when driven, making them a cleaner and more sustainable choice for our planet. And because EV batteries contain valuable elements such as nickel and lithium, they will be repurposed and recycled, reducing waste and preserving valuable resources.

Of course, the environmental benefits of EVs depend on the source of the electricity used to charge them. Tesla's commitment to sustainability and development of renewable energy generation, driving an EV powered by clean energy is becoming more accessible than ever before. By embracing innovative technologies and striving towards a greener future, Tesla is leading the charge towards a more sustainable world, where our transportation choices can make a positive impact on the environment. So let's hit the road in our EVs with confidence, knowing that we're making a difference and driving towards a brighter, more sustainable future.

Glossary of Terms

Here is a glossary of terms related to electric cars:

- **AC charging:** Alternating Current charging is the process of charging the electric car's battery from an AC electric source. This charging method is slower than DC charging, but it is more common for home charging.
- **Battery degradation:** The natural reduction in the battery's maximum capacity over time and use.
- **Battery Management System (BMS):** The system in the electric car that controls the battery and ensures optimal performance.
- **Charge Point:** A location where electric cars can charge their batteries. Charge points can be public or private.
- **DC charging:** Direct current charging is the process of charging the electric car's battery with the help of a DC electric source. This charging method is faster than AC charging and is commonly used for public fast charging.
- **Destination Charger:** A destination charger is an electric vehicle (EV) charging station installed at popular destinations such as hotels, restaurants, shopping centers, and tourist attractions. The primary purpose of a destination charger is to provide EV drivers with the convenience of charging their vehicles while they spend time at these locations. Destination chargers typically offer Level 2 charging.
- **Electric Vehicle (EV):** A vehicle that runs on an electric motor powered by rechargeable batteries, rather than a traditional internal combustion engine.

- **Fast Charging:** A charging method that uses higher power levels to quickly charge an electric car's battery. This charging method is typically used for public charging stations.
- **Hybrid Electric Vehicle (HEV):** A vehicle that uses both an internal combustion engine and an electric motor to power the car.
- **Kilowatt (kW):** A unit of power used to measure how much energy is being used or generated.
- **Kilowatt-hour (kWh):** A unit of energy used to measure the amount of energy stored in a battery or used by an electric car.
- **Level 1 charging:** The slowest form of electric car charging that uses a standard household outlet to provide AC charging.
- **Level 2 charging:** A faster form of electric car charging that uses a special EV charging station to provide AC charging.
- **Lithium-ion battery:** The most common type of battery used in electric cars due to its high energy density and long life.
- **Range anxiety:** The fear of running out of battery charge while driving, limiting the range of an electric car.
- **Regenerative braking:** A process that captures the kinetic energy of a moving car and converts it into electrical energy, which is then stored in the battery.
- **Supercharger:** A high-powered electric car charging station that can charge an electric car's battery quickly.
- **State of Charge (SoC):** The level of charge in an electric car's battery, expressed as a percentage.
- **Watt (W):** A unit of power used to measure how much energy is being used or generated.

This glossary is by no means exhaustive, but it should provide you with a better understanding of the technical terminology used in the book.

Checklist for Buying an Electric Car

❑ **Determine your budget:** Electric cars can range in price, so it's important to determine your budget before beginning your search.

❑ **Consider your driving needs:** Consider the range of the electric car you are interested in and whether it will be sufficient for your daily driving needs.

❑ **Research charging infrastructure:** Determine where the nearest charging stations are to your home or work, and consider how often you will need to use them.

❑ **Research available incentives:** Check for any local or national incentives for purchasing an electric car, such as tax credits or rebates.

❑ **Test drive multiple models:** Take multiple electric cars for a test drive to find the one that best suits your driving needs.

❑ **Consider maintenance and repair costs:** Research the costs of maintaining and repairing electric cars, as they may be different than those of traditional gas-powered cars.

❑ **Research battery lifespan:** Find out the expected lifespan of the battery in the electric car you are interested in and consider the cost of replacement.

❑ **Check safety ratings:** Research the safety ratings of the electric cars you are interested in to ensure they meet your safety standards.

❑ **Consider the environmental impact:** Remember that electric cars have a lower carbon footprint than traditional gas-powered cars, which can help reduce your overall environmental impact.

❑ **Consider the resale value:** Determine the resale value of the electric car you are interested in to ensure that it retains its value over time.

YouTube Channels

There are many YouTube channels that cover EVs. Some of the most popular ones include:

- **Fully Charged:** A popular channel that covers a wide range of EV-related topics, including reviews, news, and interviews.
- Electric Vehicle World Tour: A channel that documents the travels of a couple as they tour the world in a Tesla Model X.
- **Bjorn Nyland:** A Norwegian EV enthusiast who produces in-depth reviews and range tests of various EV models.
- The Kilowatts: A channel that focuses on the practical aspects of EV ownership, including road trips, charging infrastructure, and real-world range testing.
- **Now You Know:** A channel that covers all things Tesla, including news, reviews, and insider information.
- **Engineering Explained:** Although not specifically focused on EVs, this channel provides technical explanations of how cars work, which can be helpful for understanding the inner workings of EVs.
- **Teslanomics:** A channel that takes a data-driven approach to analyzing the EV market, including ownership costs, market trends, and the impact of EVs on the environment.
- **Car Confections:** A channel that provides in-depth reviews of various EV models, including exterior and interior features, performance, and safety.
- **Transport Evolved:** A channel that covers the latest news and trends in the EV market, including policy changes, charging infrastructure, and new models.

- **Electrek:** A news-focused channel that covers the latest developments in the EV industry, including product releases, industry news, and policy changes.

Interviews with EV Owners

Elona

YouTuber: Hi there! Can you tell us a little bit about your experience driving an electric car?

EV Owner: Sure, I'd be happy to share my experience. I've been driving my electric car for about two years now and I absolutely love it.

YouTuber: What kind of car do you have and what made you choose an electric car?

EV Owner: I have a Tesla Model 3. I chose an electric car because I wanted to reduce my carbon footprint and I was also interested in the technology.

YouTuber: What has been the biggest adjustment you've had to make when switching from a gas-powered car to an electric car?

EV Owner: I would say the biggest adjustment has been getting used to the range and making sure I have enough charge for longer trips. But with a little bit of planning, it's really not a big deal.

YouTuber: How do you charge your car?

EV Owner: I mostly charge my car at home using a Level 2 charger. It's really convenient because I can just plug it in when I get home and it's fully charged in the morning. I also use public charging stations when I'm out and about.

YouTuber: What has been your experience with public charging stations?

EV Owner: Overall, it's been pretty good. I've found that Tesla's supercharger network is really reliable and easy to use. Other public charging stations can sometimes be hit or miss, but I've found that they're improving all the time.

YouTuber: Do you have any advice for people who are thinking about buying an electric car?

EV Owner: I would definitely say do your research and make sure you understand the charging options in your area. But if you're interested in reducing your carbon footprint and embracing new technology, I would highly recommend giving an electric car a try. It's been a really great experience for me.

Jane

YouTuber: Hi, I'm here with another EV owner, Jane. Jane, can you tell us a bit about your electric car?

Jane: Hi, thanks for having me. I have a Nissan Leaf, which is an all-electric hatchback. I've had it for about two years now and I absolutely love it.

YouTuber: That's great to hear. What made you decide to switch to an electric car?

Jane: Well, I've always been interested in sustainable living and reducing my carbon footprint. When I found out about electric cars and their potential to make a real impact on the environment, I was really excited. Plus, the prospect of never having to visit a gas station again was pretty appealing.

YouTuber: I can imagine! What has your experience been?

Jane: It's been really positive. I was a bit nervous at first, especially about the range anxiety issue, but I quickly found that my Leaf has plenty of range for my daily commute and errands. Plus, I've saved a lot of money on gas and maintenance.

YouTuber: That's great to hear. What about charging? Have you found that to be a challenge?

Jane: Not really. I have a Level 2 charger installed at home, so I just plug in every night and my car is fully charged in the morning. There are also plenty of public charging options around town, so I can charge up if I need to.

YouTuber: That's good to know. What advice would you give to someone who is thinking about getting an electric car?

Jane: I would say do your research and really consider your driving needs. Make sure you choose a car with enough range for your daily routine, and check out the available charging options in your area. But overall, I would definitely recommend going electric – it's been a game changer for me.

Tom

YouTuber: Hi, can you tell us a little about your EV?

Tom: Sure! I drive a Tesla Model 3.

YouTuber: Nice choice! What made you decide to go electric?

Tom: I wanted to reduce my carbon footprint and make a positive impact on the environment. Plus, the driving experience is amazing.

YouTuber: That's great! What do you like most about your EV?

Tom: I love the instant torque and smooth acceleration. Plus, the autopilot feature is a game changer for long road trips.

YouTuber: Do you have any concerns to driving an EV?

Tom: The biggest concern for me is finding charging stations on long trips. But with the growing network of charging stations, it's becoming less of an issue.

YouTuber: Thanks for sharing your experience with us! Any final thoughts on driving an EV?

Tom: If you're considering an EV, go for it! The benefits to the environment and the driving experience are worth it.

Frank (living in an apartment)

Interviewer: Hi there! Thanks for joining me today. Can you tell us a bit about your experience as an EV owner?

Frank: Hi! Yes, I've been driving an EV for about a year now and overall, it's been a great experience. I love the fact that I'm not contributing to air pollution and that I'm doing my part to help the environment.

Interviewer: That's great to hear. I know one of the concerns for people who are considering buying an EV is that they may not have a place to charge it at home. Is that something you've dealt with?

Frank: Yes, actually. I live in an apartment building, and unfortunately, there's no way for me to charge my car here. So, I have to rely on public charging stations and the charging network provided by the car manufacturer.

Interviewer: That sounds challenging. How has your experience been with using public charging stations?

Frank: It can be a bit of a hassle, to be honest. Sometimes the stations are already in use when I arrive, so I have to wait for them to become available. And depending on where the station is located, I may have to pay a fee to use it. But, overall, it's been manageable. I just have to plan my trips and charging stops accordingly.

Interviewer: And what about the charging network provided by your car manufacturer? How has that worked for you?

Frank: It's been great. They have a network of fast-charging stations that I can use for free, and they're conveniently located near major highways and in areas where people tend to spend a lot of time. So, it's been a great option for me when I need a quick charge.

Interviewer: That's good to hear. Do you have any tips or advice for people who may be in a similar situation to you?

Frank: Definitely. I would say to plan your trips and charging stops ahead of time so that you know where the charging stations are and how long it will take to get there. And, if possible, try to take advantage of the charging network provided by your car manufacturer, as they tend to have a reliable and well-maintained network of stations.

CPSIA information can be obtained
at www.ICGtesting.com
Printed in the USA
LVHW030343250423
745266LV00003B/217